THE

Secret to Living

A   MORE FULFILLED LIFE

DOTTIE,
PRAY ALWAYS TO BE
C _____ + H _____.
BLESSINGS,
Joe Alff

Joseph Alff , MSW

To Marge,

I didn't take many shots at the target,
but I sure did hit the bull's eye.

ACKNOWLEDGEMENTS

I've learned in writing this book that, at least for me, it can't be done alone. I'm indebted to the following individuals for not only their insightful comments and editorial advice but also for their unique contributions.

To Toni Somyak, whose infectious enthusiasm infected me.

To Sidney Groeneman, who kept me sensitive to a wider readership.

To Keith Mitchell, who contributed a number of vignettes that are included in this book.

To Roy Barnes, who kept me focused on the takeaway value of the book.

To Ken Eatherly, whose superb editing clarified and polished my writing considerably.

And finally, to my dear friend Michael Denomme, who is frequently cited and quoted in this book. I doubt if this book would have been written without his continuous support. In addition to his support, he kept reminding me to remain true to my vision.

Thanks again to each of you.

AUTHOR'S NOTE

This book is a quasi-biography of who I am in the context of my career as a psychiatric counselor, and my lifelong search for the causes and remedies for human unhappiness. It was initially intended for family, friends, and future family members who may wish to know me better. What I have learned from this journey, I believe, will appeal to a larger audience.

I have attempted to portray in these pages how I view life, and how I attempt to live my life based on those views. If that comes across as preachy at times, I apologize. This is my story. Each person has his or her own story.

The names and identifying features of all of the clients and most of the other persons cited in this book have been changed for confidentiality and privacy purposes.

All proceeds from the sale of this book
will be donated to the
Grace Counseling Center, Detroit, Michigan

THE SECRET

Or, Why are some people so peaceful?

Several years ago my wife Marge and I had a new deck built on the back of our house. I was casually talking to the builder and posed this question to him, "Dave," I said, "what would you say is the single most important thing a builder must do when constructing a solid, safe, and livable structure?"

I thought he would say something like: use good materials, build a solid foundation, make sure everything is level, use excellent tools, but he didn't. He thought for a few minutes and answered, "Think water."

"Water," he said, "is the enemy. It is always trying to enter any structure, whether it comes from the sky or from the ground. The builder has to defeat this enemy. He must build a structure that will keep water out of it."

That got me thinking. Is there a single enemy to living a more fulfilled life, and if there is, what is it and what must a person do to defeat it? As I explore my own personal experiences and the lives of the numerous clients I've seen over the span of four decades as a psychiatric counselor, I think I have identified the insidious force that keeps trying to invade and destroy people's lives, and I think I know what a person can do to keep that enemy in check.

Years ago I taught a class at a local community college bravely entitled, *How To Live A Happier Life*. It was a three-hour class that combined popular music, fun exercises, and my "engaging lecture style" to convey a grab bag of motivational and positive psychological suggestions. It was well received, but I thought it lacked cohesiveness. It was a scattergun approach of techniques on how to live a happier life, rather than a more targeted approach that identified the principle reason for human unhappiness and what could be done to remedy that problem. It needed, I thought, a simple, practical approach to living that put unity into the other proactive suggestions.

Is there a single, primary cause for most human unhappiness, and if there is, what can be done about it? It seemed like a quixotic search for a very elusive quarry, yet one that has nagged at me for years.

Sometime ago I bumped into a friend at a local bookstore. The conversation soon turned to books. She recommended a book to me, adding that the members of her book club didn't like it. She said the book dealt with a person's search for "it." The elusive "it" being something very important that seems to be missing in our lives, though we're not exactly sure what "it" is. It might be happiness, purpose, love, God, etc. As the expression goes, you'll know it when you see it.

She and I found her book club's negative response to the book's subject surprising, even baffling. We agreed that the search for "it" is one of the most engaging tasks in a person's life, being both exciting in the quest and fulfilling in the accomplishment.

About a year ago, I tried to interest other members of a book club in spending some time during each meeting discussing quotes by famous persons from a book of quotations. The persons quoted ranged from the ancient Greeks and Romans to contemporary figures, such as Mark Twain and Woody Allen. The quotes covered such topics as faith, wisdom, goodness, knowledge, humor, love, piety, courage, happiness, and compassion.

I also made a similar appeal to an investment club that Marge and I belonged to for over a decade, which was being dissolved and was searching for a new theme to meet around each month.

Both groups turned the proposal down.

Again, I was baffled as to why people wouldn't be interested in exploring such intriguing topics.

Even Marge finds my interest in these topics somewhat strange. When a movie I have ordered comes to the house, she will half jokingly ask if it's another one of my heavy-themed depressing movies, which it usually is.

I generally watch them on evenings when she's away.

I mentioned these experiences to my friend Mike, explaining my confusion over the lack of interest shown by people in topics I found so intriguing. Mike, as usual, set me straight.

"Joe," he explained, "Americans are a pragmatic people. They aren't interested in looking for 'it.' They are interested in looking for a great job, a new house, the perfect spouse or partner, how to improve their golf game, how to make money, how to build the next generation of electronic devices, how to get to the moon and beyond, and those sorts of things. They aren't navel-gazers. They don't lose sleep wondering about meaning-of-life issues." He added that he and I were peculiar in that we were interested in such topics.

Americans may not display much interest in plumbing the depths of philosophical issues, but as my friend Mike pointed out, they are definitely interested in improving themselves and their environment. In fact, self-improvement is almost a national obsession.

There are two basic approaches to living: being and becoming. People in the being mode seek to live in the present. They take whatever comes their way and make the most of it. They are a pretty contented lot, sometimes too contented.

People in the becoming mode are always seeking to improve themselves, their worlds, and all too often, others around them. They are happiest when they look back on their lives and see what they have built. They are content for a short while but then jump into another project that will make something better.

The most fulfilled people live lives that are a blend of being and becoming. They enjoy the moment while at the same time are creatively involved with their worlds.

You have just tasted something that is indescribably delicious. There's a flavor in the food that you can't identify but which is perfect. You wonder what that secret ingredient is.

You observe that there are people who radiate peace. There is something special about them, and you wonder what is it about them that make them so special. What is their secret?

So are Americans interested in "it," in the secret ingredient that makes certain individuals at peace with themselves and with others? Well, yes and no. As a concept, probably not. As something concrete that will improve their lives, yes.

Convince them that "it" is a better mousetrap, and they will beat a path to your door to buy one.

"It," I believe, *is* a better mousetrap. It will improve people's lives.

Constructing that mousetrap began early in my life.

The guidance counselor at my science/business centered high school in Buffalo, New York was taken aback when I told him I intended to study psychology in college. *Where did that come from?* was written on his face. The high school didn't even offer a psychology course at the time.

After I assured him that this was indeed my intent, he offered what little advice he could on how I could pursue this career.

I dream a lot. I can't make heads-or-tails out of most of my dreams. I do, however, have one recurring dream that isn't too hard to interpret: I'm looking for something and can't find it, or I'm trying to get somewhere and can't get there. I might be in a parking structure and can't find my car; or more typically, I'm on a college campus and can't find my assigned classroom. I'm frantically searching, all the while falling farther and farther behind in my quest. I generally wake up feeling lost and defeated.

Mental health treatment is based largely on what is called psychological determinism. This theory holds that significant events, usually traumatic, that have occurred in a person's formative years will determine much of his or her subsequent adult behavior.

Sigmund Freud postulated that due to conflicted early childhood experiences people develop certain behavioral patterns that keep repeating themselves throughout the remainder of their life, even when these behaviors have become maladaptive and problematic.

The poet Edna Saint Vincent Millay put it this way, "Life isn't one damn thing after another; it's one damn thing over and over again."

A little girl may, for instance, reason that if she's an especially good girl, her father will stop drinking and abusing her mother. She takes on the responsibility of saving her parent's marriage. When this doesn't work, she spends her adult life in a series of failed marriages subconsciously reasoning, as she did as a little girl, that she can save her alcoholic and abusive husbands. It doesn't work any better in her adulthood than it did in her childhood.

The childhood influences can be simple and fairly innocuous. I knew a parent many years ago who prohibited his children from seasoning their food with salt. His parents enforced the same prohibition on him as a youngster. I wonder if he ever questioned the value of this practice, other than it was the way he was brought up.

Therapists try to help clients identify the root of their behavioral patterns in the belief that by doing so they will recognize that their behaviors are no longer needed and should be replaced with more useful behaviors.

Psychology has been criticized for spending too much time focusing on what's wrong with people and too little time on what's right with them. These critics say that mental health practitioners should be examining and building on people's strengths rather than constantly focusing on their weaknesses.

The school of Positive Psychology has developed over the past few decades in response to these criticisms. It argues, among other things, that childhood experiences need not always have a detrimental effect on the person but rather can be a stimulus for growth and creativity.

An inordinate number of great men in history, for instance, lived under the watchful eye of strong-willed women who felt frustrated in their own ambitions and who sought to achieve their dreams through a promising son. Winston Churchill, Gen. Douglas MacArthur, and Gen. George Patton come to mind.

A number of years ago, I was intently looking at works of art at the Art Institute of Chicago. I stood in front of the wild configurations of colors and shapes of a Jackson Pollack painting, intrigued but confused. I couldn't understand the painting, though I sensed that it contained something very important. I moved on to the other paintings. As I strolled through the adjoining room, I caught the Pollack painting out of the corner of my eye. I stopped in my tracks, transfixed. I saw it! It was no longer a hodgepodge of colorful splats, drippings, and explosions, but a powerful artistic expression of human experiences. I couldn't stop looking at it. It stirred something in me.

Human lives are like paintings that at first glance make little sense. Yet when we stand back and look at them from different angles and distances, we begin to see the beauty and meaning in them. The poignancy of those lives can overwhelm us.

I have been looking at the pictures of people's lives for almost forty years. With some, I saw the beauty and meaning of their lives up close, while with others I've had to stand back in time to come to those realizations.

Most readers might be thinking, "The elusive 'it' is simple; it's love." That is certainly true in a broad sense.

The parents of many of the troubled children I've worked with over the years frequently have asked me what they should do to help their children. I often replied, "Love them." I could see the confusion on their faces when I said this. Their expressions said to me, *I do love them. That's why I'm here. Something is getting in the way of that love.*

I then gave them suggestions on how to unblock that love.

It is my hope that this book will help people to unblock the love they so fiercely wish to express about themselves and to others around them.

Finally, I have sought in these pages to frame my thinking on these matters in the context of five themes.

I believe humans are engaged throughout their lives in five essential struggles. These struggles differ for each individual, with some persons struggling with perhaps one or two of the five, while others might grapple with all five, all to varying degrees of intensity. These five struggles are:

Man against Nature
Man against Man
Man against Himself
Man against Evil
Man against God

(I, of course, am using the generic "Man" here. It refers to both males and females.)

I'm presenting human behavior in the context of these struggles in order to help understand the dysfunctional modes of thinking and behaving that frequently undermine human happiness and success. If we know what goes awry in human relations, we can then, hopefully, propose and implement corrective actions. We can reveal the quality that brings fulfillment into people's lives.

That search begins in one of the deepest and scariest parts of the human mind.

Memento mori. Remember that you must die.

MAN AGAINST NATURE

Or, It begins here.

There are three or four things
I cannot understand:
How eagles fly so high
or snakes crawl on rocks,
How ships sail the ocean
or people fall in love.
Proverbs, 30: 18-20

Whether it's Yul Brynner's relentless pursuit of Richard Benjamin in the movie *Westworld* or Arnold Schwarzenegger's unstoppable stalking of Sarah Connors in the *Terminator,* the suspense and terror are unremitting. You can slow these adversaries with bullets, fire, and heavy machinery, but they just keep coming.

In the movies, the good guys win and the threat of their annihilation ends. In life, though, nature isn't so easily defeated.

Nature just keeps coming at you, again, and again, and again. Drop your defenses for a moment and it has you. You can delay it, thwart it, or try to control it, but you can never defeat it. It holds the winning cards. We're all going to die.

I can remember the scene as though it happened yesterday. The mental image of it is etched in my brain.

I was about seven or eight years old and a student at the neighborhood Catholic grammar (now known as elementary) school in Buffalo. For some reason, my classmates and I were standing outside the school. It was a bitterly cold day, even by the brutal winter standards for which Buffalo is known.

I looked across the street and saw a man lying motionless on the pavement in front of the church. I wondered how he could be so insensate to the cold. I then realized that he must be dead. Beside him knelt a woman who was cradling his head in her arms and weeping inconsolably. There were a few adults standing nearby.

The scene was both puzzling and disturbing to me.

Playing backyard basketball was my passion during my adolescent years. There was a hoop in my backyard and a flock of neighborhood kids and I played pickup basketball almost every day after school, on weekends, and during the summer. Tommy was one of those kids.

I didn't know Tommy well. I knew, or suspected, that his family was poor, and I believe he was an only child.

During a high school spring break, a drunk driver struck and killed Tommy. His parents were so overcome by grief that they were unable to attend his wake and funeral.

His parent's profound grief impacted me in much the same way as did seeing the dead person on the pavement years before: I couldn't fathom how something like this could happen.

I had worked with a female client for months and felt that I had made little headway in helping to alleviate her emotional suffering. Then, out of the blue, she walks into my office looking and acting completely different. There's a spring in her step, she's smiling and joking, and everything about her is bright and cheery.

At first, I thought it must be the result of the medications kicking in or my fine counseling taking root. I soon knew better.

She tells me that she's in love. She has found someone who cherishes her, who likes everything about her. And the feeling is mutual. She likes everything about the other person. Two people have become one, connected by their love for each other.

I push away my treatment plan for her and ride the train of love she's on. I know that nothing I can do will improve on what she now is experiencing.

Love has cured her ills, at least for now.

Rose was a meek soul who lived with her beloved dog, scratching out a bare existence in an apartment in a poorer section of Detroit. She asked little of life. That all changed one day when she stormed into my office and announced that her dog had been stolen. She would move heaven and earth to get her dog back.

She was transformed as she scoured the neighborhood for days in search of her dog. She was on a mission. Nobody dared get in her way.

I held little hope that she would succeed in her quest. I feared for her mental health when the realization that the dog was gone sank into her head.

I was, thankfully, wrong. She found her pooch and was elated.

There is no force on this green earth that is more powerful than the determination of a person to protect, find, or rescue someone they love. In Rose's case, that someone was a dog.

The power of love, even concern, works wonders. In the movie *The Russians Are Coming, the Russians Are Coming*, a Russian submarine runs aground off the New England coast at the height of the Cold War. Crewmembers go ashore to find a boat that will extricate their submarine. Their foray ends in a standoff between the Russians and the New England townsfolk. WWIII seems to be in the offing.

A little boy seeks to gain a better view of the confrontation by climbing onto the top of a house. He slips and hangs precariously from a downspout high above the ground. The Russians and Americans immediately join forces to rescue the youngster. They form a human chain up the side of the house and safely lower the youngster to the ground. The Russians and the Americans embrace each other in celebration. The celebration turns to goodwill as the townsfolk form a flotilla of fishing boats to escort the freed submarine out to sea with hearty farewells from both sides.

Whether it's a child who has fallen into an abandoned well or miners who are trapped deep in the earth, people will forget their differences and join together to save them. It's human behavior at its best.

If only that collective empathy and teamwork would work when differences and disagreements become national or international conflagration.

Over the span of my career, I have provided counseling for people whose loved ones have died. The sorrow these people were experiencing broke my heart.

I have also worked with many clients in the throes of depression. I have found that the depth of anguish is much more severe for grief-stricken clients than for those clients experiencing depression. Depression steals the pleasure of living, whereas grief takes that and more. It robs sufferers of their heart and soul. They look like ships without anchors and rudders, lost and adrift.

One of Woody Allen's movies is titled *Love and Death*. That about says it all. These are the two great emotions and issues in life. Love takes us to the heights of human experiences while grief plunges us to its depths.

I try to help the grieving clients in much the same way that I celebrate with clients who are in love: I stay with them. I toss out the treatment plan and try to walk with them through the dark and seemingly endless tunnel they are in.

When his beloved daughter Cordelia died, King Lear spoke for every grieving person when he wailed, "Why should a dog, a horse, a rat have life, and thou no breath at all? Oh, Thou'lt come no more, never, never, never, never, never. . . "

King Lear then died of a broken heart.

I always enjoyed my counseling sessions with Larry. He subsisted on disability payments, lived in poor and dangerous environments, and once got cut up in a robbery attempt. But Larry soldiered on, attending free concerts, community events, and even taking classes at the local community college.

He lived scorned by his father, who never stopped comparing him unfavorably with his only sibling, a brother who owned a successful insurance agency. His father couldn't understand why Larry couldn't "get it together" and be more like his brother.

His father's scorn was offset by his mother's love. She accepted Larry for who he was and always supported him throughout his difficult life.

Larry's mother died. Larry tried to cope with her death but couldn't. He told me he also wanted to die so that he could be in heaven with his mother and Jesus.

Like King Lear, life finally broke Larry, and he soon died.

Glenn was a huge Black man who filled the doorway when he entered a room. He was also as gentle as a lamb. He came from a family of African American Christian preachers and biblical scholars. He wanted to be like them but his lifelong struggle with schizophrenia precluded that route for his life. He, like Larry, lived on the fringes of society, living on disability benefits. The combination of psychotropic medications and weekly counseling with me kept the demons that bedeviled Glenn at bay, and he functioned fairly well, given his mental and emotional limitations.

The Wellness Plan, where I worked, decided to contract out its Social and Mental Health Services Department to the community mental health agency. That meant that the psychiatrist and I would no longer be treating Glenn. I told him about this change, but he didn't seem to hear what I was saying. I called Glenn a few times after the change had occurred to see how he was doing. He wasn't the same Glenn. It was as if he hardly knew me.

Glenn couldn't adjust to the change.

I learned that about six months after Glenn's case was transferred, he barricaded himself in his apartment and was acting bizarrely. The police surrounded the apartment and told him to come out peacefully. Glenn came rushing out holding something black. The police shot him dead.

He was holding a Bible in his hand.

Much of my career has been spent helping clients control the destructive forces in their nature. These were clients who suffered from a wide range of addictions and emotional and thought disorders. The roots of many of these disorders seemed to lie in their genes. Their family histories were laced with the same disorders.

Like *The Terminator*, their addictions and emotional and thought disorders kept coming at them. I would routinely encourage these clients to enter a Twelve

Step Program, which provides ongoing support to help people control their addictions, whether it be to alcohol, drugs, food, sex, pornography, spending, etc. They are reminded that they are one slip-up away from being consumed by their addictions.

Marlene was a kind, soft-spoken, and gentle soul. She had never fully recovered from the death of her father when she was eight years old. He had showered her with love and protection.

As a single mother, she raised her children well and they were all successful. She should have spent the closing years of her life in relative contentment and comfort. She, however, had a history of bipolar disorder and lived in fear of experiencing another prolonged depression.

It had been years since the last depressive bout, and she and I hoped that the combination of psychotropic medications and counseling would keep it that way.

It didn't happen.

She became severely depressed and had to be psychiatrically hospitalized. She later went to live with her son and his family. She was finally placed in a home for the elderly. She died about a year later.

The demon of bipolar disorder beat her.

Memento Mori is inscribed on one side of the coin. *Memento Vivere* is inscribed on the other side. *Memento*

Vivere means, "Remember that you have to live," or, "Remember to live."

Many times, the demons in the closet aren't who we think they are.

My friend Mike had a recurring dream where he was being pursued by a shadowy figure. It was a disturbing dream.

One night, the dream changed. The dark figure showed himself. It was the actor Vincent Price. He wasn't sinister or menacing at all. In fact, he smiled at Mike, as if to say, *You have nothing to fear from me.*

Mike said the dream stopped after that.

Woody Allen said that he doesn't mind dying; he just doesn't want to be there when it happens.

I have counseled a few clients over the years who either were in the presence of someone who had died or they themselves had a near-death experience. The accounts of their experiences would allay Woody Allen's fears. As one client, who survived a near fatal heart attack, informed me, "I will never fear death again."

Our physical demise is always an elephant in the room, but humans live under other clouds that darken the sunshine of joyful living. These clouds can be grief, fears, insecurities, disappointments, physical or mental limitations, and/or one of the worst, concerns for loved ones.

Woody Allen states that there are two groups of people in the world: the horrible and the miserable. The horrible are people who are blind, crippled, deformed, poor, or afflicted with other horrible conditions, while the miserable are people who worry all the time that they will become horrible.

Most people deal with these pains by sweeping them under the carpet and dancing over them. This works up to a point, though tucked in the back of their minds is the fear that they could become horrible at any time.

Some people, on the other hand, throw back the carpet, look their fears straight in the eye, and are surprised at what they see.

St. Francis of Assisi was morbidly afraid of leprosy and avoided anyone who had it. He finally conquered this life-draining fear when he forced himself to embrace a leper.

I have found in my clinical practice that just about everyone fears failure and rejection. We want to be right and liked all the time. I certainly have these fears.

I have informed a couple dozen people that I'm writing this book. A cold chill has come over me numerous times, thinking that this book will be a bust and that the people reading it will take a negative view of me.

I have asked God to guide my mind, heart, and hand so that it will be successful. I wonder if my goal and God's goal for me are one and the same. I'm asking Him for what I want, while He might decide to give me what I need.

I *want* a good book. I *need* to know that people will continue to love me, regardless of what they think of this book.

Everyone has "lepers" in their life – things that scare them and which they avoid. They, like St. Francis, must eventually face up to their fears if they wish to overcome them and live fruitful lives.

Joseph Cardinal Bernardin, the late cardinal of the Catholic diocese of Chicago, said that he feared two things in his life: being falsely accused of something and having cancer. Both those things happened to him. And both those things brought him closer to others and to God.

Instead of always avoiding our fears, it may be wiser to step into them. We may find that they are the portals for deeper understanding and richer relationships.

Stepping into our fears takes considerable courage and faith, faith in God and in ourselves. It's going through doors without knowing what lies behind them. I believe people will be pleasantly surprised at what they find behind those doors.

Humans like to control things. They generally gain that control by analyzing and offering explanations of the world around them. Describing how things work may serve utilitarian purposes, but it frequently robs people of mystery and wonder.

I like art museums. Occasionally, I will be standing by a parent who is describing a work of art to their child. As their explanation goes on, the wonder in the child's eyes fades and is replaced with boredom. The child is ready to bolt out of the museum after about ten explanations, determined never to return.

I will look at a painting and marvel at how the artist can convey an image with such poignancy and power. I feel a sense of awe when I listen to the musical compositions of Chopin, Bach's Mass in B Minor, a Mahler symphony, and many, many other incredible works of music. I will frequently put down a book and marvel at how a writer can create such beautifully crafted prose. I marvel at how historians can amass so much information and then present this mountain of facts in such an interesting and informative way. I'm amazed at what a great athlete can do. I once saw an Olympic figure skating medallist perform live, and I was awed by his skills. It's something that can't be fully appreciated by watching such performances on television.

I can't fathom how every human face is different. All there is to work with are two eyes, a nose, mouth, chin, and cheeks. How many different ways can six components be shaped? Yet every face is distinctive. Snowflakes! Each one is geometrically perfect, beautifully designed and different. There must be quadrillions of them, maybe in just one big snowfall. You can explain the physics of these things to me all day long, and I will still think that they just can't happen. The list goes on: blades of grass, leaves, the human ear, and fingerprints. They all seem to me to be incredible mysteries—nay, miracles.

I'm in awe of the Universe. Distances are measured in light years. Light goes around the earth 7.7 times in a single second. Distances in space are measured in light years to seemingly endless powers. The distances are mind-boggling.

I read that only about 5 percent of the universe is visible, while the remaining 95 percent consists of dark matter and dark energy that can't be seen or directly measured.

How can such immense power be released when something as small as an atom is split, and how on earth did humans figure out how to do it?

I look at a limb of a tree that must weigh tons and wonder how it stays affixed to the trunk.

I'm in awe over many man-made things. I look at a jumbo jet and can't imagine how something that large can get aloft and stay in the sky for hours. I look at a microchip that is the size of a fingernail and marvel at how much information it contains.

Explaining the physics to me is akin to explaining a masterpiece painting to a child. The wonder of it is far bigger than the explanation.

I marvel that Marge loves me, or that family and friends display so much care for me when I've been ill. I can't fully understand forgiveness.

I'm amazed that I've made it through life. I'm not very smart, nor am I a very hard worker. I also have a tendency to say dumb things, yet I've been able to keep jobs and do some good along the way.

As the King of Siam said in the musical *The King and I*, "Tis a puzzlement."

A few people have told me that when they know they are dying, they will kill themselves first. They don't wish to go through the agony and humiliation of the dying process, nor do they want to burden their loved ones. Life, however, affords no greater opportunity for people to show their love for others than to care for them as they die.

If only we realized that we are all dying and that we should love others as if these were their last days on this earth.

Treating death as a friend rather than an enemy is a great idea and practice, and hopefully, people will come to that point when the time is right, but every instinct in our body tells us to run as fast as we can when the Grim Reaper is approaching, or lacking that, to fight it for all we're worth. Self-preservation runs deep in the human soul. We will protect and defend ourselves when we feel our survival is at stake.

The problem occurs when we stay in that survival mode even when we're in no apparent danger. We act like every encounter is a life-and-death issue where we must show our supremacy. We subconsciously believe that we will cease to exist if we let down our guard. We want to be like God because God is immortal. God never dies. He is also all knowing. Nobody messes with God. We want to be all knowing. We must always win. Nobody messes with people who are always right, even death, or so the subconscious mind thinks.

Our search for the basic cause for human unhappiness now moves us into the arena of human relationships and the faulty notions we have about ourselves.

MAN AGAINST MAN

Or, If you want a friend in politics, get a dog.
Most things in life are politics.

My older brother Dave and I were assigned by our father to paint the first and second floor hallways and the connecting staircase in our house. We split up the work and set out to paint our respective areas. After a few days, I saw that Dave was progressing faster with his section than I was, and I realized that at that pace he would finish ahead of me.

I concluded that this was because he had tricked me into letting him do the easier half. I vehemently protested.

After much arguing, we agreed to swap the areas we were working on. He would take the area I had, and I would take the area he had.

We resumed painting, and in a few days I again noticed that he was progressing faster than I was and would finish sooner.

I again got mad at him, only this time there was nothing I could say about it. I therefore did the next best thing: I hoped he would spill a can of paint on the carpet.

My wife and I belonged to an investment club for many years that had twelve members and met monthly, up to a year ago when it was dissolved. The format for the meetings consisted of contributing fifty dollars, per member per meeting, and agreeing on which stocks to buy and sell. The primary purpose of the club was socialization built around learning some of the ins and outs of investing. We each had our own family or individual portfolios that constituted our primary investments. Club members frequently mentioned investment decisions they had made in their own portfolios with the implied message that their portfolios were well managed and substantial. I think over the twelve-year existence of the club, we all tried to learn who had the largest portfolios.

The game is to allude to how large your portfolio is without being specific as to its overall value.

We were in competition with each other without seeming to be competitive.

I once said to a friend, "John, I have two questions for you. How much do you make, and how much sex are you getting?" He thought for a few minutes and answered, "A lot and a little. And I'm not telling you which is which."

So it goes with men. It's bad form to seem competitive, yet we are. It's a game most of us play.

Oscar Wilde put it this way, "It's not enough that I succeed; my friends must fail."

I was playing a psychotherapeutic game with a teenager whom I was counseling that required the players to answer questions of a personal nature. She drew a question that asked what she would request if she was granted a special power. She said that she would like to know what other people are thinking. I remarked that she would probably find that information rather upsetting. People may be all smiles on the outside, but beneath those friendly faces lies an awful lot of envy, jealousy, lust, anger, and even hatred.

Probably the most commonly asked questions one person asks another person is: Where do you live? and, What do you do for a living?

These two questions almost always put me in a quandary.

If an out-of-town person asks me the first question, should my answer be Detroit or Grosse Pointe? Detroit has no cachet, while Grosse Pointe definitely does. I've had three choices in answering the second question, prior to retirement: I'm an administrator for an HMO Mental Health Department, a psychiatric counselor, or a psychiatric social worker. Each of these answers has decreasing levels of cachet.

I sense that the degree of acceptance or rejection I'll receive will depend largely on the answers I give.

I also sense that those questions pose a moral dilemma for me: Do I puff myself up by going with Grosse Pointe for the first question, and mental health administrator or psychiatric counselor for the second question; or do I go the more humble and honest route with Detroit and psychiatric social worker? Do I play to my audience, or do I stay true to myself?

I've grown tired of the hackneyed interchange, "How are you?" "Fine." I prefer replacing, "Fine" with, "God is good."

African Americans will generally respond to the latter with, "All the time," while White people will usually look at me like I'm some sort of religious fanatic.

Like the decision to be honest with where I live and what I do for a living, I feel that I'm being asked to make a moral decision.

This decision, I believe, lies at the heart of the human soul: Should a person be true and honest to him or herself even when it runs the risk of being rejected by others? Do I have the courage to be who I am?

People have a false self and a true self. The false self is how we want the world to see us: It's a lot of window dressing. The true self says, *Here I am; take it or leave it.*

Interestingly, people are much more attracted to the true self, for they admire people who are comfortable with who they are. They wish they could be like that.

Human beings don't like to lose. I know: Ask anyone who has played tennis with me and they'll tell you what lies behind my seemingly laid-back demeanor.

I was playing tennis with an old buddy during the period that followed being laid off from the Wellness Plan, and I was trying to figure out where to go with my life. I said to him that I was considering becoming an Episcopal priest, as people frequently comment on my religiosity.

"Those people have never seen you on the court," replied my friend, alluding to my competitiveness in tennis, replete with expletives when the game isn't going my way.

I have always loved competitive activities, both as a participant and as a speculator. I have learned also that competition is a double-edged sword. It's like alcohol; it's great up to a point, then it becomes counterproductive and even dangerous. A player crosses that line when winning becomes a necessity: When it's not enough just to beat an opponent; you must always beat him or her convincingly. You no longer play the sport for enjoyment, but to prove something. When it defines your worth.

I mentioned earlier that I taught the class *How To Live A Happier Life* for a number of years. I always enjoyed the compliments I received following the class, but I crossed the line from enjoying the compliments to needing them. They became like a mood enhancing drug to me, and I was becoming addicted. The class was meant to help people, not to inflate my ego. I didn't like the emotional strain it was putting on me, including sleeplessness and anxiety prior to each class.

I stopped conducting the class when I realized the adverse effect it was having on me.

This issue of competition, winning and having to prove myself came to a head early in my professional career when Wayne came into my office for counseling.

Wayne and I were meant for each other at the time. We both had something to prove.

Wayne viewed his life as a complete failure. He once had a promising career as a semi-professional baseball and hockey player, and he was married with children. A lifelong addiction to alcohol changed all that, cutting short his athletic career and robbing him of family and friends.

Now it was taking his life. If he didn't quit, he was told, he would soon be dead.

The abyss I was looking into was different, and almost as scary to me. It was the loss of a dream and a future.

I had recently received a Masters of Social Work (MSW) degree from Wayne State University in Detroit, Michigan and was flush with confidence as I started my career as a psychiatric social worker for a Detroit area health maintenance organization that served Medicaid recipients. I had the romantic notion that I would lead the patients who came to me out of the wilderness of their confused thoughts, troubled emotions, and complicated social situations, with my good heart and the skills that I had learned.

Graduate school provided me with a treatment model that was a tidy package of beginning—diagnosis of the condition and development of a treatment plan, middle—execution of that plan, and end—patient problems are significantly reduced or eliminated, with the patients and therapist happily parting ways.

That was how it was supposed to work. Only it didn't.

Doctors weren't referring the patients I thought they should be referring; many patients who started treatment with me stopped coming after a few appointments; a few patients always kept their appointments but displayed little progress toward achieving the treatment goals; and the interdisciplinary approach to patient care that was so highly-touted in graduate school was ne'r to be found.

I was starting the first season of my career expecting to hit home runs, and I was instead barely drawing a few base-on-balls.

My optimism, which had turned to frustration and anger at times, was in danger of morphing into disillusionment and depression. The honeymoon, if there was one, was over for me.

I sought some comfort and understanding from friends. Instead of speaking forthrightly about my frustrations, I shrouded my concerns in humor. I spoke about founding a school of psychotherapy known as Accolade Therapy, where well-placed compliments would dispel the patients' problems, or Get-A-Grip Therapy, where patients are sternly told to buck-up and fight the good fight. "Good God, I can carve a better man out of a banana," were my pretended sobering words to these patients.

I was hoping that they would see through my frustrations and disappointment and offer me words of encouragement. Their comments instead suggested to me that I wasn't up to the job.

Enter Wayne.

As I said, we both needed to put some points on the scoreboard. He needed to quit drinking, and I needed to feel that I was helping him do that.

We liked each other well enough and settled into a comfortable working relationship. We usually began the sessions talking about sports and other shared interests before getting down to the business of how to keep Wayne sober. We explored his life and history of alcoholism—the torturous road of failed treatments and losses—and then developed a plan of action full of substitute behaviors and supports that would prove effective this time: all the things the textbooks tell you will work.

They didn't work. Wayne always kept his appointments and was surprisingly honest in reporting his continued drinking. Each session, I strove to shore up his motivation, but to no avail.

Finally I said to him, "Wayne, what can I do for you?"

"Nothing, Joe," he answered.

We knew it was over. I continued to see Wayne. We talked less about controlling his drinking and more about the pleasant moments in his life. These were actually very enjoyable sessions.

Wayne died a few months later of complications from alcoholism.

Put another zero on the scoreboard for me, I thought.

We all have ego defense mechanisms that protect us from feelings of inadequacy. Sometimes, an arrow slips through the armor and the hurt starts. We are forced to look ourselves in the mirror and ask some very difficult questions.

This moment of truth had arrived for me.

No more dodging, denying, and distorting. I needed honest answers.

Why were so many of my patients dropping out of therapy? Why weren't more patients achieving the treatment goals set out for them? Why weren't the doctors referring more patients to me? Had I made a mistake pursuing this career? How on earth would I start over, and what else could I do for a living?

I then listed in my mind those things of which I was certain:

I always wanted to be a psychiatric counselor.

I believed God had made a way for me to become one.

I cared deeply for my patients and always gave them my best.

I never intentionally did anything to harm them.

I sensed that I had helped a few of them, even though those successes weren't always overtly evident.

That was enough for me. I would stay the course, only this time with a different perspective and attitude, one that I believed would make me both a better therapist and a better person. I would no longer keep looking at the scoreboard. I would give each patient who I saw my very best, and I would stop agonizing over whether it met some idealized outcome.

Outcomes, I came to realize later, can be very misleading in psychiatric treatment.

Certainly, I would always work on improving my clinical skills through continued studying and peer reviews, but that was different from harshly scoring and scolding myself.

I refused to compare my clinical performance against those of other therapists who seemed to be doing better than I was doing. They are they; I am I. They bring their talents to what they do; I bring my talents to what I do. They work well with some patients while I work well with others. There's enough pie to go around.

No more trying to show people how smart or accomplished I am. That's a big part of the comparison game of which I was dropping out.

It was Liberation Day for me.

These realizations freed me for the rest of my life. I not only stopped competing with other therapists but I now viewed most of them very favorably, telling them how much I admired their work, which I meant.

More importantly, I viewed my clients with equal admiration. "If I was dealt the hand you've been dealt in life, I would be dead by now," I sincerely told them. "Life keeps knocking you down, and you keep getting up. I don't think I could do that. I would have given up long ago."

Many people who I used to view as competitors became my heroes.

Interestingly, I learned some time later that research shows that 50 percent of all psychiatric patients discontinue treatment after three visits, feeling satisfied with the symptom relief that the few sessions provided them. Studies have also shown that almost all patients view any amount of psychiatric treatment as worthwhile while the therapists providing the treatment generally feel that more could and should have been provided.

This information might have allayed the feelings of inadequacy I had at the time.

I am grateful that I didn't have this information then. It may have prevented me from being liberated from the tyranny of having to always prove myself.

In the end, Wayne and I didn't get the victories we sought, but we got the victories we *needed*. I got the monkey of perfectionism and competition off my back, and he got a companion to walk with him during the last days of his life.

Years ago, I played tennis regularly with a bunch of friends. Mike was one of them. Mike wasn't impressive on the tennis court. While the rest of us were decked out in snappy tennis apparel, Mike usually stepped on to the court wearing mismatched shirts and shorts, complete with—of all things—black socks. Whereas we took hefty swings at the ball, Mike punched at it. You just knew this guy was easy pickings.

Fat chance. Nobody could beat him.

But what was even more puzzling about Mike and his tennis game was what happened after he beat us. He was always full of compliments for his opponent's game. To listen to Mike, you would have thought he lost the match, rather than the other way around. I, for one, never felt so good about losing.

I'm told that one of the secrets to the car manufacturer Toyota's success is how they employ Mike's tennis behavior on a corporate scale. You hardly know they are there, yet when the final sale numbers are rung up, Bingo, they're leading the pack.

No one envied Mike's tennis game. I think that's the way Mike wanted it. That, and quietly winning.

There was one other thing that was interesting about Mike. If you said to him, "Mike, how do you do it? How do you win so much?" he probably would have responded, "Beats me. There's really nothing great about my tennis game."

Red Auerbach, the legendary coach of the Boston Celtics, once described his player Sam Jones this way, "Sam isn't my best scorer. He's not my best rebounder. He's not even my best defensive player. All I know about Sam is that when I put him into the game, our score goes up real fast."

Players like Sam Jones bring something to the game that can't be found in statistics. Their presence brings out the best in their teammates, and with it, a lot of victories.

If asked to identify some of today's premier basketball players, few people would identify the former Detroit Piston and current Denver Nugget player, Chauncey Billups. He's an outstanding player, but he's much more. He ignites teams that win. He brings attention to his teammates, not to himself. He knows how to tap into their potential and abilities. He makes everyone a winner.

Why do humans engage in so much unhealthy competition? How did we get that way? Can anything be done to free us from its bondage? A close look at how some people remain trapped while others break free from always having to glorify themselves should help to provide the answer.

MAN AGAINST HIMSELF

Or, It's still the same old story,
a fight for love and glory.

Now he told a parable to those who were invited, when he marked how they chose the places of honor, saying to them, "When you are invited by any one to a marriage feast, do not sit down in a place of honor, lest a more eminent man than you be invited by him; and he who invited in you both will come and say to you, 'Give place to this man,' and then you will begin with shame to take the lowest place. But when you are invited, go and sit in the lowest place, so that when your host comes he may say to you, 'Friend, go up higher;' then you will be honored in the presence of all who sit at the table. **For every one who exalts himself will be humbled, and he who humbles himself will be exalted.**"

Luke 14: 7-12

The Secret To Living A More Fulfilled Life

For whoever would save his life will lose it, and whoever loses his life for my sake will find it.
Matthew 16: 25-26

I have always found these biblical passages both intriguing and confusing. When we exalt ourselves, we end up being humbled, and when we humble ourselves, we end up being exalted. And even more confusing is the notion that in seeking to save ourselves, we lose ourselves, while in losing ourselves, we save ourselves.

Self-preservation and self-aggrandizement, and their close cousins, self-justification, self-righteousness, blaming, faultfinding, and scapegoating, are as innate to humans as our need for food, drink, sleep, and sex.

Throw a stick in any direction and you'll hit dozens of people who are trying to puff themselves up by showing how smart, funny, or skilled they are to others.

It's all so evolutionary. Smart and/or attractive people seeking out other smart and/or attractive people in order to have smart and/or attractive kids who will move human societies forward. Isn't that how the world works?

Humbling ourselves isn't something that comes naturally or easily to us. In fact, it's questionable whether it can be achieved at all. It runs against our evolutionary grain. Yet Scripture tells us that this is the road to human happiness and success. It's a nice concept, but it sorely needs a good working definition.

Answer these questions, I've concluded, and I've solved a big piece of the puzzle in how people can live a more fulfilled life.

I worked for over ten years as a mental health consultant for Head Start programs. Head Start is an enriched social and learning experience for children three to five years old who are from disadvantaged homes.

I have often said that if you don't like three-to-five-year old children, you probably don't like humanity. Humankind doesn't get any better than these joyful, playful, trusting, and loving children. That even includes the children who I worked with who had a variety of behavior problems, such as problems sitting and standing still, following directions, paying attention, turn-taking, and sharing.

When I entered the classroom, these children would run up and shout, "Mr. Alff, Mr. Alff, Mr. Alff," as they scrambled to hug me. It was much the same with any other adult.

Three days a week, I would go from the Head Start programs during the day to counsel teenagers in the early evening. What a difference!

There was no joyful eagerness on the faces of the teenagers who came into my office. They looked like they were en route to their execution. They didn't think they needed counseling and resented having to see me.

Many of them would stonewall me during the sessions by only reluctantly volunteering information. Many of these sessions were unbearably long for me, and I assume also for them.

What happened, I wondered? How did those fun-loving, trusting preschoolers turn into sullen and unhappy teenagers?

I concluded it was girls — in a manner of speaking — and raging teenage hormones. In preschool, there were no differences between boys and girls. They interacted freely and playfully. Then the girls get shapely and pretty, and the boys take notice. The Dating Game is on. Girls compete with other girls for attractiveness, and boys compete with each other for the girls' attention. Their focus turns inward. Windows to view the outside world become mirrors to view only themselves.

Narcissism takes root. They get into the habit of exalting themselves, and in turn belittling their peers. The *joie de vivre* that was so much a part of their lives a few short years before slowly disappears.

It would be nice to report that it's a development stage that ends with the passage of the adolescent years. But regrettably it doesn't. As the song, *As Time Goes By,* states, "It's still the same old story, a fight for love and glory." That fight seems to go on and on and on.

It seems like a rotten way for the species to continue.

I was dropping my son, Chris, off at high school on a very cold Michigan winter morning. As our car approached the school, I noticed another student who was walking. He was dressed in a light jacket that was partially opened and he wore loafers with no socks. He was dressed more for a spring day rather than the bitterly cold winter day that it was.

He should have been shivering from head to toe and double stepping for the front doors of the school, but he wasn't. In fact, he was sauntering along as if he didn't have a care in the world.

He was looking cool, not cold, as he intended.

When teenagers are trying to exalt themselves by looking cool or hip, they are oblivious to what's going on around them, even the bitter cold. They are locked into their own narrow world.

I wondered what the large wooden boxes of boots, gloves, and sundry other clothing items were for at the middle school where I was working. Was the school planning a clothing drive?

I was informed that the boxes contained clothes that the students had left behind and had not recovered.

Most of the students in this school district were from poor families, and their parents surely didn't have the means to replace so many clothing items. I also wondered how the students at the school managed to lose those clothes. Wouldn't they have noticed the minute they stepped outside on a cold afternoon that they were missing something important?

Yet they walked home without a jacket, boots, or gloves. When their parents asked them about the whereabouts of the item, they probably answered, "I don't know."

And they didn't know. They were much too busy trying to exalt themselves by looking cool and hip to notice the absent clothes. They probably couldn't understand why their parents were getting so angry with them.

Given this type of behavior, the human population of northern climates should have died off prematurely from pneumonia before it had a chance at procreation. That's assuming that the parents didn't kill their teenage children first.

Steve was menacing. He was a short African American male whose muscles bulged out of his shirt and tapered pants. His whole body language shouted, *Don't mess with me*. He was referred for counseling by the courts for anger management.

I didn't welcome having him as a client. Detroit had far too many angry African American males with chips on their shoulders. They didn't make for clients who were open to self-examination and personal change.

Steve, however, surprised me. After a few sessions of displaying resentment for having to be there, he began to let down his guard. He spoke about being a little kid on the block and having to protect himself from bullies. He frequently lay in bed at night listening to his parents shout at each other and was fearful that his father's temper would spill over onto him. Steve had spent time in prison, where any sign of weakness meant subjugation and humiliation.

Steve was tired of being a patsy and of living in fear. His muscles and don't-you-dare-mess-with-me demeanor would change that. He would defend himself with his frightening presence. Every human encounter was for him a matter of self-preservation that went back a long way.

It was an all-day trip from Detroit to Wisconsin, where our children were attending college. Our friend Dan drove the van while his wife Carol talked, and talked, and talked. She pretty much talked throughout the long trip. We could have passed the most magnificent natural wonder, and I doubt if Carol would have noticed it. She was far too busy exalting herself with accounts of her life and experiences.

This is too bad because Carol is a delightful person, and what she has to say is generally very interesting. One wishes that she would stop every now and then and take in the world around her. She needs to have occasional NOW-WOW! moments.

I feel the same way about people who are always taking pictures. They need to occasionally put down their cameras and experience the view.

The department psychiatrist and I were treating Jon for schizophrenia. He was prescribing psychotropic medications, and I was providing counseling. This treatment went a long way in controlling the auditory hallucinations that plagued Jon, but not entirely.

Jon lived in a nearby halfway house, and I occasionally saw him walking the streets. He always walked in a peculiar manner, swinging his arms and moving his legs in an awkward way. He told me that he walked this way in an attempt to control "the voices."

When he walked down the street, all he could think about was his body movements. Like Carol, teen-agers, and most people, he was so preoccupied with himself that he was oblivious of his surroundings.

Jon wasn't interested in what was happening around him. He was interested in surviving his frightening hallucinations.

Shortly after receiving my MSW and beginning my career with The Wellness Plan, I excitedly told the head of the Pediatrics Department that I wanted to form a parenting group for interested Medicaid plan members. His response startled me. "Joe," he said, "these women have so many problems, they couldn't begin to relate to their children."

"These women" were certainly hurting, which was the reason I wanted to start the group. Each day, they faced roadblocks of poverty, single parenthood, and feeling that society disapproved of them. These battles drained them of most of their energy, leaving little for their children, whom they dearly loved.

Always working on surviving takes a lot of work, leaving little energy for anything else.

The human species was continuing through these women and their children, but that was about it. They were not getting much satisfaction out of life.

Some people do a great job at exalting themselves, maybe too well.

She came into my office dressed to the nines and glittering with very expensive jewelry. She cried throughout the interview as she told me about her emotional misery while living in the lap of luxury. Her husband displayed nothing but contempt for her and was constantly belittling her. Her children were beginning to do the same. She yearned to leave the marriage but couldn't bring herself to surrendering the sumptuous lifestyle she was living.

She was trapped in her own self-glorification.

A priest once informed his parishioners that he wished the church had a dollar for every person who told him that they would be happy if they only had money, as well as for every person who told him that they would give away all of their money if they could only be happy.

Dr. Sims was an African American internist and nephrologist who was highly esteemed throughout the entire Detroit medical community. He was my primary care physician. He diagnosed me with hypertension and prescribed medications to control it. He said that he also had hypertension but seldom told anyone. I asked him why. He said it was a sign of weakness and would tarnish his reputation.

I wondered what else he was hiding from people around him.

He, too, was trapped in his own self-glorification.

People are pretty good at creating and burnishing an impressive image, only to sense that they are trapped in a world of pretenses and false friendships. Celebrities, of course, immediately come to mind. I once read that Joseph Heller, author of the classic book *Catch 22*, lived in fear of being introduced to someone who didn't know who he was. After all, who wants to know Joe Heller, the plumber who lives down the street?

Certainly not the prettiest girls on the block. There's no genetic future for that Joe Heller.

After twenty years of being Director of The Wellness Plan's Social and Mental Health Services Department, the medical director and I had a falling out over staff productivity, and I was demoted to being a psychiatric social worker, the duties of which already comprised about seventy percent of my time.

I wondered if I was merely demoted or had contracted leprosy by the way people avoided me. I guess having a title gave me a certain amount of power that attracted people to me. Now that I didn't have it, I was passé. My stock in the human genetic pool was definitely trading at an all-time low. I, on the other hand, learned who my true friends were.

Some people begin to suspect that always trying to be the most desirable animal in the herd isn't working and that it is, in fact, counterproductive to their happiness and prosperity. A new approach for living is called for.

Maybe the meek actually do inherit the earth.

Mavis was part of a group I facilitated at The Wellness Plan to provide help and support to women who were having difficulty coping with everyday stresses. She told the group that her stepfather physically and sexually abused her as a child. For most of her life, she harbored an unquenchable hatred for this man. This hatred probably served her well for much of her life, in that it kept her sane and alive, but that period of self-preservation had passed long ago. It was now working against her, robbing her of the ability to relate positively to others and to enjoy the pleasures of life. She knew she had to rid herself of this hatred.

She turned to God for help.

For seven years, Mavis asked God to remove her virulent hatred. One day, while at work, it left her, and she knew it. She began to sing and dance around the workplace. She was full of joy. Her co-workers thought Mavis had lost her mind, but her supervisor knew better. He told them to leave Mavis alone.

Not only did the hatred leave her, but it was replaced with a sense of compassion for her abuser. She renewed contact with him and even sent him presents on his birthday and on Christmas.

Mavis had found life again. To do this, she had to stop trying to save herself from a battle that was over decades ago, and to see life in a whole new way.

Phil was engaged for years in a fierce battle with his next-door neighbors over a fence they had installed that he didn't like. The battle probably started in his childhood when his short stature and shy disposition made him feel vulnerable.

He wasn't going to feel small and powerless this time. This time, he would stand up for himself.

The dispute dragged through administrative and legal court hearings. He became increasingly obsessed with it, severely hampering his ability to relax and enjoy life.

Phil finally realized that to win he had to lose. He instructed his attorney to cease the litigation and give his neighbors what they wanted.

Phil saved himself when he stopped having to protect himself.

Some people show us what life is like when we stop trying to impress the world with who we are, when we put down the mirrors, and our interest shifts from ourselves to the world around us.

It was such an unusual experience that my friend Mike was eager to tell me about it. He said he was attending a banquet and was seated next to a professor from the University of Pennsylvania. He described him as a bona fide intellectual with an impressive resume of academic credentials, professional achievements, and honors bestowed on him.

If anyone could bask in his glory, it was this professor. Yet he spent their whole time together querying Mike about every facet of his work. He took delight in who other people are and not in himself.

I was watching a TV show decades ago that examined the workings of the Vatican. Pope John XXIII was the pontiff at the time, and as part of the show, the moderator interviewed him. The moderator mentioned at the beginning of the interview that the pope was recently named Man Of The Year by *TIME* magazine for his work in modernizing the Catholic Church through the Second Vatican Council he had convoked.

I expected the pope to talk about his efforts and achievements in this area, with at least a hint of a hey-look-at-me attitude. He didn't. In fact, he didn't seem the least bit interested in his achievements. He instead asked the moderator if he had any children, and learning that he did, asked for their names. One of them was Kevin. The pope asked what Kevin was like. The moderator, looking surprised at this turn of the interview, briefly described his son.

I watched in amazement. This important person was much more interested in a little boy he had never met than in the accolades that the world was showering on him. Is it any wonder Pope John XXIII is being considered for sainthood?

If anyone should have been preoccupied with survival, it was my friend Bob. He was dying from Lou Gehrig's disease. The muscles throughout his body were slowly shutting down as he marched toward certain death.

I would call Bob regularly at his home near Seattle, and once visited with him for a week.

Bob was part of a Christian ministry team that went regularly to a nearby prison to bring the Good News of Jesus Christ to the prisoners. Whenever I spoke with him on the phone, he rarely talked about his illness but instead joyfully spoke about all the good things that were happening with the prisoners through his ministry.

Toward the end of his life, he told me he could no longer leave his bed. He said that this didn't bring an end to his ministry. He said that when telephone solicitors called he would ask if they attended church. He said that this question would open the door for many wonderful discussions about faith.

Richard would have none of this namby-pamby, live-outside-of-yourself, behavior. He made it clear where he stood in the battle for the survival of the fittest.

I worked for a year at a suburban Detroit middle school where Richard taught, and I was assigned to improving the academic and behavioral performances of some of the most disinterested and poorly achieving students in the school. Two months into the program, I discovered that the principal planned to cancel my program at the end of the school year and use the funds for other purposes.

I was devastated. I had left a job that I thoroughly enjoyed and didn't relish the thought of having to restart my career again. I was also angry at the principal's duplicity.

The day after learning this upsetting news, I was talking to Richard. Richard was viewed as a curmudgeon by many of his fellow teachers. I enjoyed his cranky manner and often found him to be strikingly candid and rather funny.

I told him that something terrible had happened to me. Before I could elaborate on the content of my distress, he bluntly asked, "Does it have anything to do with me?"

"Well no, Richard," I replied.

"Then I don't care," he said.

I had to laugh. It was so Richard.

That's one of the things I liked about him. He said things that social conventions won't allow many of us to say.

Does Richard speak for most of us? Are people focused primarily on "numero uno" and only marginally interested in others? Is "meism" the order of the day?

Over the past year, I have told at least two dozen people that I'm writing this book and have frequently brought it up in conversations. I can count on my one hand the number of times someone has said to me, "Joe, how's your book going?"

Years ago, two friends visited with Marge and me after attending a weekend family gathering. They had come all the way from Maine to Michigan for the event. They were hurt and angry when they told us that, during those two days, not a single family member asked them about their life in Maine.

People fervently believe that they are interested in others. By and large, they aren't. They want to talk about themselves.

Talking about ourselves comes natural and easily while taking an interest in others and listening is often times hard work. It takes discipline to do it.

The game of golf, I assert, is a metaphor for human interactions.

A golf foursome gathers together for three to four hours with each player playing his or her individual game. Each player is focused on their own game and only tangentially on the other players' performances. The conversation between holes and shots is minimal and shallow: "Where do you live?" "What do you do for a living?" "Nice shot." and a few cursory follow-up comments.

At the finish of this "social gathering," each player has two concerns: What is my final score, and how does it compare with the scores of the other three players? Knowing anything important about the other players is incidental.

This, heaven forbid, goes on week after week, both on or off golf courses.

Self-preservation and self-aggrandizement have five kissing cousins. They are self-justification, self-righteousness, blaming, faultfinding, and scapegoating.

My friend Dick once told me that when human beings are gone from this planet, a huge sign should be placed on it with the inscription:

HERE LIVED HUMAN BEINGS
THE GREAT RATIONALIZERS

I would probably add another sign. This one would read:

HERE LIVED HUMAN BEINGS
THE GREAT BLAMERS

Corey was one of the youngsters in the Boys Hope/Girls Hope program in Detroit. Boys Hope/Girls Hope is an international, privately funded program that provides youngsters who are at risk of slipping into wasted lives with a family-like living experience in residential homes with supportive house parents, a quality high school education, tutors, counselors, and a guaranteed college education. I was one of the counselors.

Corey was a very likable young man. He was an African American teenager who could talk endlessly about basketball and most other topics but shied away from addressing such sensitive issues as his absentee father. He was like many other African American youngsters who I saw in counseling; he saw himself as the next Kobe Bryant, playing in the NBA.

Corey was frequently excluded from school for disruptive behavior. I could see that he had attention deficit disorder with hyperactivity. I informed him of this diagnosis and proposed that we work on it. He blew off this proposal. To show him that my diagnosis was correct, I proposed a challenge to him. I placed a pen in front of him and challenged him not to touch it for ten minutes while we talked. He gladly accepted the challenge. I placed my watch on the table that separated us and soon said, "Go." In a few minutes, Corey became restless and began tossing the pen up into the air, well before the ten minutes had elapsed.

"There, Corey," I said, "that proves that you have ADHD."

He still wasn't buying it, telling me that he could have held off touching the pen but simply decided not to.

I took a new tack. I asked him which facets of his basketball game needed improving.

"None," he replied.

"None," I said, incredulously. "You mean to tell me that every facet of your game is perfect?"

"Yes," he insisted.

Nothing I could say could shake his belief in the perfection of his basketball game.

Corey came from an environment where survival dictated that he show no weaknesses, and that included any defects in his school behavior, or in his case, in his basketball game. He also needed to shine, and living in the belief that he would be an NBA star filled that need. And it certainly wasn't cool or hip to tell his peers that he was in counseling. So trying to convince him he was flawed in any way wasn't going to work.

This denial severely hampered Corey's chances for success. He continued to have behavioral problems in school and was difficult to coach on the high school basketball team. He barely completed high school, and I doubt he ever played organized basketball again.

I haven't seen Corey in many years. If I did, I suspect he would still be convinced of his perfection and would be resistant to any need for improvements in his life. If I asked him about his lack of success in going beyond high school or in becoming an NBA basketball player, he would probably tell me that he could have done it but decided not to, or he would blame his teachers or coaches for undermining his efforts.

Teenagers are the masters of self-justification. They can be caught red-handed doing something wrong and will argue with the finesse of a Philadelphia lawyer that they didn't do it, or failing that, why they shouldn't be punished.

I have repeatedly told teenagers who found themselves in such situations that the solution to their troubles is simple. Just say to your accuser, "I did it. I'm sorry. I will try not to do I it again," and then accept the consequences for your actions.

They look at me like I'm crazy. They genuinely don't believe they have done anything wrong.

My high school had just won the city Catholic basketball championship. I was a bench-warming member of the school's team. I joined in with my classmates that evening in celebrating. The next morning, my father noticed that I wasn't ready to go to school. He asked me why, and I told him that the players of the team were given the day off.

Later that morning, the school office called our house and asked why I wasn't in school. My mother passed on what I had told my father earlier that day.

The next day I found myself in the vice principal's office, asked to explain my obvious falsehood. I rambled on with one justification after another that either proclaimed my innocence or mitigated my guilt.

The vice principal finally asked me if I knew what the word "rationalization" meant, for that was what I was doing. I was piling on one rationalization after another that morning.

It's not the crime that gets people in the most trouble; it's the cover-up. But when you look at the faces of people who have done wrong, they seem bewildered that anyone would even suggest any wrongdoing on their part.

Self-preservation and glorification means steadfastly believing in our own righteousness.

I once presented to about fifteen people two simple statements that required an either yes or no answer:

I'm a nice person.

I'm an honest person.

Everyone responded "yes" to both statements, though a few people would have preferred to use the qualifier, generally. Two respondents got angry with me for even posing the question to them.

I'm sure if I had asked the same two questions to prison inmates, I would have received the same overwhelmingly affirmative responses.

It seems America is wasting a colossal amount of money with its judicial and prison system because virtually everyone in America is nice and honest. Why, I question, are we locking up so many nice and honest people?

I once asked a room of about ten fairly fundamental Christian believers if any of them have ever done anything in their life that harmed another person. They all answered "no."

These are people who have dedicated their lives to a faith whose foundation is the redemption of sinful behaviors, yet none of them saw themselves as sinners. They might see themselves as sinners in the abstract, but not in the concrete.

(Poor misguided Jesus, if He had only known that His sacrifice on the cross was for nothing.)

Virtually everyone thinks he or she is a safe driver. It makes me wonder why there are so many vehicle accidents. I suspect the auto insurance companies are cooking the statistics in order to goose their rates.

Does anyone change his or her political sentiments? Does anyone truly listen to the other side, seeking to understand rather than to rebuke? Does anyone remotely consider that his or her political views might be a tad incorrect? I suppose there are a few people like that. I would like to meet them. I would vote for them if they ran for political office. Of course, their opponents would say that they are wishy-washy. I much prefer flexibility and adaptability to intransigence. Woe to the person who never questions his or her convictions.

Many of those convictions, as noted earlier in this book, stem from childhood influences and go uncontested throughout a person's life. The mental tapes keep playing on and on.

My nephew Keith tells of when he and his girlfriend from Northern Ireland were in America watching TV and listened to a report of a power outage a few miles away from his apartment. She informed him that "outage" is not a real word while he insisted that it was. She returned home and consulted the British Oxford English Dictionary and it wasn't there. He consulted the New American Dictionary, after she had left, and it was in that dictionary, along with the annotation, "Americanism."

They were both right.

Sydney Harris, the deceased Chicago columnist, once said that the problem with the debate over abortion is that both sides are right. The same thing can be said about the questions of gay marriage and affirmative action; both sides are right.

Yet people, families, even nations, will go to the mat over issues where all parties firmly believe that they are right, and indeed both frequently are.

Does that mean that people shouldn't stand up for what they believe is right? They certainly should stand up for their convictions and be counted. They should also seek to understand the other side of the issue. That is how acceptable compromises are achieved.

Marge and I probably have an equal number of Republican and Democratic friends and acquaintances, many of who are fiercely committed to their political positions. Though I have my political preferences and occasionally express them, I believe I understand and am often sympathetic to opposing viewpoints. I have, in fact, even changed some of my thinking over the years.

I don't believe the world would be a better place if it subscribed to and practiced everything that I believe is right. I, at least, wouldn't want to live in that world.

I have enjoyed many books, movies and food dishes that were recommended to me which I initially discredited.

People like to reduce complex problems to ten-word statements of moral outrage, as if simplicity is the hallmark of truth. Life would be a lot easier were issues that simple, but alas, it isn't.

John F. Kennedy once said that most issues are varying shades of gray. Lee Iacocca said that he goes with a decision when he feels 70 percent sure of the outcome. Seventy percent for him is about as close as he will get to certainty.

In the movie, *Gran Torino,* the central character Walt is about as mean-spirited and insulting as an individual can be. Toward the end of the movie, he decides to confess his sins to his parish priest. He confesses to a few minor transgressions, including failure to pay a small tax. The priest, who is well aware of Walt's history of offensive behavior, appears bewildered by Walt's weak confession.

He shouldn't be. Walt is Everyman when it comes to an examination of conscience. We deny, minimize, or justify our transgressions. We genuinely don't see ourselves as being sinners. We dismiss our faults while exaggerating those of others. "I'm going to heaven when I die," is the thinking; "and others probably won't."

> None of us know our faults.
> Forgive me when I sin without knowing it.
> Psalm 19:12

Convincing people that they did anything wrong is as futile as my trying to convince Corey that he was hyperactive or needed to improve his basketball game.

St. Isaac the Syrian said, "It is a greater miracle for a man to see his sins than it is to raise the dead."

Seeing our faults is akin to the numerous times I've proofread the various manuscripts for this book. I very carefully read each sentence in search of errors. I correct the mistakes I find and am convinced that it's ninety-eight percent error-free when I'm finished. I then turn it over to proofreaders who find two to three times as many mistakes than I found and corrected.

It's very difficult for me (and I presume for other writers) to see my mistakes, and to ask for constructive criticism. It is much easier to say that the product is perfect and be done with it. Yet it is only through such feedback that a person can identify his or her errors, whether in writing a book or living a life, and then to work on eliminating them.

But alas, people aren't generally disposed to such feedback. They prefer to point fingers. So if things go wrong (which happens all the time) and I'm not responsible, then who is responsible? It must be the other person. Blame the other person: It makes perfect sense.

I'm glad I've never done much couples counseling. These sessions are battlegrounds, with each person throwing accusations at the other, and neither party admitting that they have contributed to the marital discord and unhappiness in any significant way. He or she might own up to a few minor personal faults, but these are nothing compared to the egregious shortcomings of the other person. "You change, and then we'll do just fine," is the message each person conveys.

I have never heard a divorcee admit to contributing to the ruination of their former marriage. They are quick to point out to the listener(s) what their former spouse did or didn't do that could no longer be tolerated. I'm sure if I spoke with their former spouse, I would get the same finger pointing.

Wouldn't it be nice to hear someone say, "I was difficult to live with." But then, the people who can say that are probably the best ones to live with.

The staff meeting had just finished. A few of the therapists and support staff remained afterward in the conference room. I was one of them. A therapist said that she had been seeing a male client for a few sessions and determined that it would be best if he saw a male therapist. She turned to the clinic director, who was also a therapist, and implored him to take the case. He declined. She then turned to the staff psychologist, who was male, and made a similar request. He also declined. That left me as the only remaining male therapist in the clinic. The three of them went round and round about what to do, never turning to me to ask if I would like to see the client, which I would have gladly done.

I felt smaller and smaller as their discussion continued. I couldn't leave the room fast enough. I was hurt to the core. It took me a couple of years to get over that hurt.

Now here's the truly remarkable thing about that episode: I have known these three people for years. They are some of the nicest, kindest, most Christian individuals I have ever known. They have been nothing but supportive toward me over these years. They would never knowingly do anything to hurt me. Yet they did.

People don't mean to hurt other people, but they do exactly that all the time.

Marge and I were recently visiting with friends who have a son in college. In the course of our conversation, the father said that he had just read a paper their son had sent them from college. The son was very proud of it. The mother said that she had not read it. I got the feeling that she didn't intend to read it.

I'm sure she loves her son and wouldn't do anything intentionally to hurt him, yet she's hurting him by not taking an interest in something that is very important to him.

The opposite of love isn't hatred; the opposite of love is ignoring people, which is something people do all the time. We commit sins of omission rather than commission. We neglect and ignore others. We don't answer e-mails, phone calls, or even listen to others when they have something to say. We treat others like they don't exist. Husbands don't notice when wives change their hairstyle, wear a new dress, or are upset over a work problem. Wives fail to affirm husbands when they stumble through a project. There would be far fewer divorces in America if spouses and partners paid more attention to each other, and far less human misery in the world if people sincerely sought to understand others.

In the movie *Alfie*, Alfie, played by Michael Caine, says he never meant to hurt anyone. To this his friend replies, "But you have, Alfie, you have."

People think that not intending to hurt others vindicates their harmful actions. Practically no one rises in the morning intent on harming others, yet we may go to bed at night leaving many hurt feelings in our wake.

The police stopped a friend of mine, years ago, for driving under the influence of alcohol. He refused to take a Breathalyzer test. He was taken to the police station, booked, and put in a cell until his wife could pick him up. Upon entering the station, he noticed a wall camera that was trained on him. He realized that he was being filmed, and that the film would be used as evidence in court to prove that he was inebriated. He therefore put on his best I-am-sober act. He was confident that his act had succeeded. The court hearing arrived, and indeed, the film was entered and shown as evidence. He saw himself on the film, incontestably drunk. Case closed. He admitted his guilt and accepted the consequences.

"Iron Mike" Tyson, the professional heavyweight boxer, made this revealing comment after watching the documentary *Tyson*, "I never used to understand why people saw me as such a monster. And then I saw the movie, and it all made sense."

I wonder what people would think if confronted with video evidence of their daily encounters with others. Would they, like my friend and Mike Tyson, scrap their self-justifications and silently bow their heads?

People will think that because they are successful they are absolved from being nice. I once saw a cartoon that showed two individuals in hell with flames all around them. The one person said to the other person, "I don't know why I'm here; my obit in the *New York Times* was two columns long."

I take our family cars to a service station near our house for maintenance and repairs. Mike works the front: pumping gas, checking oil, fluids and tire pressure, writing work orders, and calling customers when the work is completed. Mike always greets me enthusiastically and makes me feel good. I'm observed that he's that way with all the customers. He radiates kindness.

Mike once asked me to pray for him. I immediately thought it would be for a personal problem. He instead asked me to pray that he would never do anything that is harmful to another person.

I thought to myself, "There's a person who possesses spiritual wisdom."

There's a story about a soul who is at the gates of heaven, where an angel asks him if he wants to go to heaven or hell. He asks what's the difference. The angel escorts him down a hallway and has him look into two rooms. The first room is full of people seated around a banquet table full of wonderful things to eat and drink. The people around the table have implements attached to their arms and hands that allow them to grasp the food and beverages, but are a few inches too long to allow them to put the items into their mouths. Everyone in this room keeps trying to eat and drink the delicious food and beverages but keeps missing their mouths. They are getting more and more frustrated, hungry, and angry with themselves and with everyone around them. It's a very unhappy scene.

The angel then takes the soul to the second room. The setting is exactly the same as in the other room except for one difference. Instead of everyone unsuccessfully trying to feed him or herself, they are successfully feeding each other. Everyone in this room is happy.

The angel says the first room is hell, and the second room is heaven.

Most people don't reside exclusively in one or the other room. People tend to shuffle between the two. They will at times be intent on justifying their actions, even when they are clearly wrong, but will at other times be quick to apologize for their wrongdoings and seek forgiveness. They will eagerly glorify themselves with boastful comments and supercilious attitudes but will then sincerely downplay their skills and achievement and seek to give credit to others. They can be eager to find fault with others and to heap blame on them for their mistakes but will at other times see only the good in them and dismiss their shortcomings. They move from ignoring others to embracing them, from discouraging people around them to validating and affirming them.

Nothing flies in the face of self-glorification more than having to apologize for our misbehavior. This is because it means acknowledging that we aren't always right and that we do things that hurt others. It is a crack in our delusion of self-righteousness. It is better to ascribe the problems to other people, holding them responsible.

I've had three occasions within the past six months where friends have told me of conflicts they were having with family members or other people. Each time, I advised them to apologize to the other person for their behavior. You would have thought that I had suggested they jump in Lake Michigan in January. They bristled at the very idea. One friend stated, "My apologies don't come that easily." I suspect that his apologies don't come at all. Another one, who is a devout Christian, informed me that reaching out to the offended person and apologizing would *not* be the Christian thing to do!

It's tough to apologize to an individual, and it's even tougher to apologize to a whole group of people, many of whom are not aware of your wrongful behavior.

A few years ago, I was a member of our church's search committee to call a new rector. It soon became apparent in the committee's deliberations that a deep divide existed as to the selection of a candidate. The liberal versus conservative rift reflected the same division that existed throughout the worldwide Anglican/Episcopal church community. Both sides were passionate in their convictions.

The divisions and hurt feelings that subsequently arose didn't disappear with the selection of a new rector. As a result, the church retained a consulting company that specialized in facilitating the healing process in broken parishes. This included conducting a parish-wide meeting that provided the parishioners with the opportunity to express their thoughts, feelings, and experiences.

With considerable trepidation, I arose at the meeting and acknowledged to everyone present that during the selection process I had thought, said, and done things that I suspected had hurt others. I asked their forgiveness. I then sat down. I was half hoping that this would open the door for others to seek forgiveness and for a general healing to occur. That didn't happen, though I felt healed.

Marge and I were recently visiting with one of my sisters and her husband. They hosted a family gathering that included a surprise birthday celebration for me. As I was about to cut the cake, I told everyone that the greatest gift they have given to me over the years was their forgiveness and how they have stuck with me when I have behaved badly.

Just as apologizing comes hard for most people, forgiving those who have wronged us is equally difficult. People find it strangely comforting to hold on to perceived and real slights and mistreatments. "I'm unhappy because of what that awful person did to me." We surrender ownership for our happiness.

Booker T. Washington said, "I will permit no man to narrow and degrade my soul by making me hate him."

Mohandas Gandhi said, "The weak can never forgive. Forgiveness is the attribute of the strong."

People sometimes say, "I can forgive, but I can't forget." Forgiveness without forgetting is pretty hollow.

As Director of The Wellness Plan's Social and Mental Health Services Department, I was an easy administrator. It was a small department with a very competent professional and support staff who knew their jobs and did them well.

Late one afternoon, I glanced at the therapists' schedules for the next day and noticed that Sallie, the substance abuse counselor, had blocked out time on her schedule. She was standing nearby, and I asked her for an explanation. She said that she needed the time to do her paperwork.

This issue had surfaced in the past, and I had made it clear to all the staff therapists that the department experienced enough patient no-shows to allow each of them to complete their paperwork at those times. I didn't tell them that the medical director was constantly complaining to me about what he viewed as the staff's low productivity. I always defended the staff, but his point wasn't unreasonable.

As Sallie was persisting in her justifications, my anger rose and finally exploded.

"Damn it, Sallie," I shouted, "I told you not to do it, and I meant it. Don't do it again."

I'm sure she and everyone else in hearing distance were shocked by my outburst. None of them had ever seen this dark side of my nature.

Some months later, Sallie told me that my outburst so frightened her that she was afraid of seeing me the next day, for fear that it would continue.

She was completely taken aback when I passed her in the office the following morning and greeted her with a smile and a pleasant, "Good morning, Sallie." She said that I acted as though nothing had happened the previous day.

When Marge and I were in the WSU School of Social Work, the faculty and students attended a spring retreat in a rustic Michigan setting for an extended weekend of seminars and recreation. During one of the evenings with her, I made a jerk out of myself with some unwelcome advances.

I arose the next morning, convinced that she wouldn't want to ever see me again, and I didn't blame her. Much to my astonishment, she walked into the cottage where I was staying and greeted me as if nothing had happened the previous night. She didn't show a trace of anger or resentment toward me. She, in fact, looked delighted to see me. I felt like the Prodigal Son when he saw his father running to him as he was returning home.

She has done that over and over again throughout our marriage: forgiving me and forgetting. She has her say, lets go of it, and moves on.

It's one of the many things I love about her, and which she has taught me: forgive and forget.

The actress and singer Marlene Dietrich spoke for men and women when she said, "Once a woman has forgiven a man, she must not reheat his sins for breakfast."

The Episcopal Church, like many other Christian churches, begins each liturgy with the General Confession in which we confess that we have not loved God with our whole hearts, have not loved our neighbors as ourselves, and we have followed too much the desires and devices of our own hearts. That act of contrition prepares us for the Great Feast that follows.

I believe this is a good mindset to have throughout the day: being aware that I can intentionally or unintentionally, by my thoughts, words, and deeds, hurt people throughout the day. This awareness, I believe, helps to lessen these hurtful moments. It keeps my guard up against them.

Humans aren't particularly built to forgive and to forget. Even when they know that their anger is eating them alive, and that they must release it in order to be content, they still can't do it. The internal rage continues. Can, and should, people forgive and forget particularly grievous crimes committed against them; such as, rape, murder of a loved one, or a fraud that has robbed them of their life savings?

I believe there is only one way to achieve lasting forgiveness, regardless of the severity of the harm done to a person. I remind myself that I'm capable of committing any crime under certain circumstances. I look at prison inmates and think that I could be in their place.

As a young man, for instance, I frequently drove while legally intoxicated. What if I had struck and seriously injured or even killed someone while driving in that condition? Am I any less guilty because it didn't happen? I don't think so.

Decades ago I did something in a rage that could have seriously injured or killed two people who were very important to me. That terrible outcome didn't occur. Am I any less guilty because it didn't happen? I don't think so.

I couldn't begin to count the number of times in my life when I have ignored people, or through my thoughtless and selfish actions diminished their worth as human beings.

It's difficult to condemn people, and it helps in forgiving them their offences against us, when we realize that they are we and we are they.

An old friend of mine, the Rev. Greg Sammons, once wondered aloud to me what goes through children's minds when they see their parents in prayer. They must view their parents as super humans who are all-knowing and all-powerful, and who control the world around them. Yet here they are in humble submission to someone more knowing and powerful than they are.

I'm not sure what children think at these occasions, but I suspect that the impact on them is very beneficial.

I have known a number of children from families with very successful fathers, and have treated a number of clients from such families. I have found that many of these children grow up with significant emotional and behavioral impairments. It's as if their individual personalities never developed.

I wonder if those problems would have been prevented if they realized that their parents had feet of clay, that behind the powerful veneer is a person who worries, is insecure at times, and makes mistakes, and that their parents are combinations of strengths and weaknesses, achievements and blunders, love and insensitivities.

There's a story about a psychiatrist who was addressing a room full of mental health practitioners. He announced that he could get any patient to open up to him. They would tell him personal secrets that they had never revealed to anyone else in their life. Members of the audience tried to guess the psychiatrist's incredible technique. None could. The speaker finally fessed up. "It's easy," he said, "I tell them my secrets."

I always find it amazing how effective this is. I recently mentioned to my neighbor/friend a mix-up Marge and I experienced while trying to connect upon her return to Detroit from Chicago. He reported that he and his wife had a similar mishap. Mention a medical problem you're having, and most likely, the listeners will report similar personal experiences or someone they know who has had a similar problem.

People, as I stated earlier in this book, want to put aside their false self and to reveal their true self—warts and all. It can take just one honest individual making a few honest statements for genuine communications to begin.

I half-jokingly, half-seriously tell people that if they're feeling down on humanity the remedy is to pull their car over to the side of the road and pop the hood. A crowd will quickly form, providing them with advice and assistance.

While driving, Marge and I have broken down a number of times in Detroit. Detroiters unfailingly came to our assistance. For all the knocks Detroit gets, Detroiters are some of the kindest and most helpful people in the nation.

There are approximately 150 different types of psychiatric treatment, and none has proven more successful than the twelve-step programs. Alcoholics Anonymous is the best known of these, though there are twelve-step programs for virtually every form of addiction.

Its success lies, I believe, in its humanity. There is no finger pointing, self-justification, rationalization, or self-glorification in a twelve-step meeting. The participants must admit to everyone there that they are addicts and that they have made a mess of their lives and the lives of other people.

Their self-awareness and honesty bind them together and create a medium for living addiction-free lives.

I was fifty-five when I found myself unemployed and needing to restart my career. It wasn't an easy task. I flirted with the idea of muddling along to age fifty-nine and a half to start drawing on my IRA account, and then to sixty-two to draw early Social Security benefits. That made sense in my head but not in my heart. I knew I had a lot of good things I could still do as a therapist, and I wanted to draw on over twenty-five years of professional experience to continue to help people. I asked God to lead the way.

It took a few years of fits and starts, but I finally ended up working with troubled teens and children in various professional settings. Those last ten years of my career proved to be some of the most satisfying working years of my life.

If I wanted to find a new job, I needed to tell people that I was unemployed and to ask for their assistance. That wasn't easy to do when you live in a community that seemingly defines a person's value by the status of his or her employment.

Many of the people who came through for me surprised me. I barely knew some of them, yet they called me regularly with leads. There is a special place in my heart and prayers for those people who assisted me when I was down.

In order to experience that love, I needed to be vulnerable. I needed to allow people to help me.

In Woody Allen's Academy Award winning movie *Annie Hall*, Woody and Annie, played by Diane Keaton, are waiting in line to see a movie. Standing behind them is a man who is explaining to his girlfriend the communication theories of Marshall McLuhan. Woody thinks he's a big windbag and is getting more nauseous by the moment hearing him pontificating. He finally turns to him and tells him what he thinks of him. The man states that he's a college professor who teaches communications, which proves that he knows what he's talking about. Allen asks, "Oh, yeah?" and pulls Marshall McLuhan out from behind a movie poster. McLuhan tells the young man that he has been listening to what he has been saying about his communication theories and states that he doesn't understand his theories at all. Woody Allen sighs and comments to the audience that everything in life should end that easily.

I wonder how much better off the man would have been if he acknowledged that the communication theories of Marshall McLuhan are complex and that this was his limited understanding of them.

Bertrand Russell, the British mathematician and philosopher, said, "The whole problem with the world is that fools and fanatics are always so certain of themselves, but wiser people so full of doubt."

There's a book and a movie that details the Enron collapse titled, *The Smartest Guys in the Room*. Another book that describes how America got entangled in the Vietnam War is titled, *The Best and the Brightest*.

I have been in many meetings in my career and heard what the "smartest guys and gals" in the room have to say. They tend to complicate everything with their elaborate analyses and endless objections. What they say seems to be so right that no one dares to question them. They get promoted and move up the corporate ladder.

There is only one problem with this scenario: The fruits of their labors are often rotten. Departments, companies, and corporations crumble under their management, yet boards and corporate officers continue to hire, support, and promote them.

Dr. P was the psychiatrist for The Wellness Plan's Social and Mental Health Services Department for about twenty years. He provided the perfect blend of spending time with clients, successfully treating them, and working with the department psychiatric social workers and support staff. Under his administrative and clinical direction, the department ran smooth as silk.

Enter Dr. M. He was fresh out of medical school and psychiatric residency. He wrote the most beautiful and impressive psychiatric assessments and treatment plans. He even typed them on his laptop computer and personally placed them in the clients' medical charts.

I'm sure when the medical staff looked at Dr. P's and Dr. M's psychiatric reports they observed the marked contrast between Dr. P's brief scribbled notes and Dr. M's elaborately typed notes. Dr. M was probably to their minds the much better clinician.

The administration must have thought so; they made Dr. M the clinical head of the department, bypassing the twenty-year contributions Dr. P had made.

Dr. M didn't see much value in the department psychiatric social workers, so he didn't use them very much in treating clients. He also spent a lot of time with clients in order to write those finely crafted clinical reports. This resulted in frequent backlogs of clients who became increasingly upset and angry by the long delays to see Dr. M. Dr. M felt the pressure of the full and angry waiting room and became explosive with the support staff, and even with clients at times. The support staff was caught in the middle, their nerves fraying. It was a total mess.

The department went from smooth running under Dr. P to chaos under Dr. M. Many clients left the office in worse emotional condition than when they had arrived. The staff was also breaking down. After two years of this disorganization and unhappiness, the administration contracted the whole department out to the Community Mental Health Agency. Everyone lost their jobs.

Dr. M probably went on to a new psychiatric position, writing beautiful clinical notes that continued to impress everyone. He's probably been put in charge of departments, maybe even organizations. I suspect those departments and organizations aren't faring any better under his management than my former department did. And everyone is looking in all the wrong places to explain the problems: It couldn't be Dr. M, who writes such wonderful clinical notes.

Nobody would mistake me for being one of the smartest people in the room. And I will be the first to admit to my blunders.

I tell people that I keep a running list entitled, *What Was I Thinking?* It includes: buying two cars at about the same time that were the same model, year, and color; planting a tree branch on the front lawn and thinking it would grow into a tree; having a couple of beers prior to being interviewed for a college admission (I must have smelled like a brewery; I wasn't accepted.); buying a decrepit ladder and using it (a rung broke while I was on it, which could have maimed or killed me); being convinced that George McGovern would defeat Richard Nixon for the presidency (Nixon won in a landslide); making a comment at an important meeting in the military that completely undermined what the head of the mental health unit was attempting to do; arguing that *The Shining* was an excellent movie; wearing pants for years that were about an inch or more too short; wearing a beloved plaid jacket until I saw another person wearing the exact same jacket and thinking how ridiculous he looked; and putting on so much cologne at my son's wedding that I smelled up the room.

I keep another list entitled, *Things I Scoffed At And Ended Up Loving.* This list includes: jogging, iPods, going to church, cruise control on cars (first demonstrated to me in city driving), Coney Island hot dogs, individually wrapped slices of cheese, Christmas letters, baseball, and traditional furniture.

It is so easy and supercilious to scoff at things. People feel superior when they look down their noses at what other people find enjoyable or attractive. *They have no taste or smarts, while I do,* is the message. It's a not-so-subtle form of self-aggrandizement and self-righteousness.

Does that mean that everything is relative, that there are no absolutes or standards of excellence? A Monet painting is certainly better than a cartoon drawing. A classic French dinner is superior to mac-and-cheese. We can acknowledge and appreciate the finer things in life without thinking we are the arbitrators of those choices or to diminish the enjoyment people get out of whatever they consider beautiful, worthwhile, or just plain fun. In fact, it's fun to be lowbrow every now and then.

My friend Mike again came through on this issue. He once said that everyone should enjoy some junk and silliness in their lives. For him it was the silly TV show *Married With Children*. My brother-in-law delights in reading comics, performing magic tricks, and letting loose with a good loud burp every now and then.

I'm a sucker for fifties and sixties rock-and-roll songs. I go so far as to put my iPod in my ears and take over for the singer, to the riotous delights of my imagined screaming audience. That includes telling the audience that they are wonderful and the stage manager informing them that, "Joey Alff has left the building."

I love April Fools Day. I once had my family and friends in a tizzy when I informed them that I had decided to pursue seminary studies to become an Episcopal priest.

The next year, I informed them that Marge and I were joining the Peace Corps, (They were on to me this time).

Mark Twain said, "The first of April is the day we remember what we are the other 364 days of the year."

I think one of the reasons I enjoyed working with children so much, and why I was so effective with them, is because I could be silly with them. Children are delighted when adults act silly. Maybe one of the tonics for human unhappiness is to dress up like a clown every now and then, and then to act like one.

Whenever I'm certain of something or think I'm on the side of the angels on some issue, I remind myself of the many dumb and foolish things I've said and done in my life and how many times I have been wrong about something or someone. This brings me back down to earth.

I recently watched the movie, *Harvey*, (mentioned a number of times here) for perhaps the sixth time. I noticed that I had mistakenly credited the wrong scenes to some of the Ellwood P. Dowd quotes I've used. If I hadn't seen the movie again, I would have sworn that I remembered those scenes correctly.

Whenever I'm confronted with a problem, whether it's a leaky faucet, making an investment, treating a patient problem, or how to cook a certain dish, I frequently approach these problems the same way. I put on my, "Ah shucks, I don't know" hat and ask people what would they do. Everyone has an opinion and enjoys giving it. I then sort through the opinions I've gotten and implement what I think are the best ones. I invariably get great results using this technique.

I'm not very smart. A review of my high school and college grades will show that. But I am good at asking for people's opinions and then choosing the best ones. Not only have I solved the problems, but I've also brightened people's days by asking their opinions and thanking them afterwards for their great advice.

One of my strengths lies, I believe, in being able to cut to the chase and to get things done.

As Director of The Wellness Plan's Social and Mental Health Services Department, I reasoned that to run my department I had to achieve three simple things: 1) Keep the clients happy. 2) Keep the staff happy. 3) Make money for the company.

I achieved those objectives. I can't recall a single client complaint registered against the department in over twenty years. The staff was like family. And the department was one of the most profitable in the company.

I think a lot of people thought I should be more serious, attend more meetings, and write more reports.

Keep things simple is my motto. Clutter and complications create stress and inefficiencies. Jeff Bezos, the founder and CEO of Amazon.com, is fond of saying that his company must do three things in order to succeed. They are:

1) Provide low-cost products. 2) Offer a wide selection. 3) Service the orders in a speedy and friendly manner.

He's a person after my own heart. He keeps things simple.

At the two places where I worked with teenagers, I think I was viewed as a simplistic thinker. I identified myself as a cognitive-behavioral therapist who focused on clients' erroneous thoughts, perceptions, and behaviors as the source of their troubles.

In therapy, I sought to reframe a person's thinking by pointing out such mental distortions as jumping to conclusions, overgeneralizations, all-or-nothing thinking, personalization, minimization, labeling, and magnification.

I was frequently encouraged to "go deeper" with the youngsters. I reasoned that improved thinking resulted in improved behaviors that netted improved self-esteem, which is what these teens needed the most.

In the end, the thinking seemed to be, "Give Joe the uncomplicated cases."

Yet I believe I had one of the best client return rates, client satisfaction, and when it was measured, one of the best client outcomes.

Not bad for a simplistic thinker.

I was so shy in high school, college, and beyond that I rarely dated. The line in the family was, "Who's going to take in uncle Joe this Christmas?" Sad uncle Joe ended up with the best spouse in the world and a home life that couldn't have been better.

"Ah, shucks, I don't know how it happened: lucky I guess."

In the investment club Marge and I belonged to, I believe I was perceived as the weak link in terms of my input at those meetings. That may be because the club was about investing in individual stocks, which I thought was a bad idea. My investment philosophy was simple: dollar cost average, buy established mutual funds with proven records of success, diversify, asset allocate, keep your costs down, and draw on yields in retirement. Those practices didn't take a lot of smarts.

I have a dear friend who plays the, "Ah shucks, I don't know" routine to a T, maybe too well. To listen to him, he's not sure how to tie his own shoes. I was with him and another friend once when the other friend wondered how Michael managed to succeed in his career. Mike turned to this friend and in an irritated tone informed him that he has two Masters degrees, a Ph.D., was a college instructor, has written a book on Shakespeare, and manages social services programs throughout the country that service and employ hundreds of people.

In other words, "Don't be fooled by my modesty. I'm a whole lot smarter than you think I am."

Humility, as will be explained later in this book, must be coupled with self-appreciation for the gifts each person possesses, develops and gives to the world. Mike in this episode needed to perform that personal affirmation in a public way.

One of my favorite movies is *Harvey*. It stars Jimmy Stewart, who plays Ellwood P. Dowd, a kindhearted but seemingly befuddled soul who converses with his invisible friend Harvey, a large white rabbit. His family views him as an embarrassment, and they seek to have him committed to a psychiatric facility. In the end, Ellwood and Harvey prevail as others accept both of them, and even want Harvey to themselves.

The psychiatrist who owns the facility can't figure Ellwood out. He finally says to him, "Dowd, who are you?"

Ellwood answers, "Years ago, my mother used to say to me, 'Ellwood . . . in this world, you must be oh so smart or oh so pleasant.' Well, for years I was smart. I recommend pleasant."

I keep reminding myself that nice is better than smart. Not much gets done proving how smart you are, while all sorts of wonderful things get done proving how smart other people are.

John Powell, S.J., Ph.D., is a Jesuit priest and psychologist who has written a number of best-selling psychology books. In a set of tapes, he spoke about a time when he was addressing an assembly of fellow Jesuits. He was eager to impress them. As he waited to take the podium, he scanned the faces in the audience. He saw priests who were struggling with addictions, others who were experiencing chronic pain, and others who were unpopular college lecturers. He felt God had opened his eyes and his heart at that moment with a simple message: *I don't want another performance; I want an act of love.*

Fr. Powell realized that those suffering priests didn't need to know how good he is; they needed to know how good they are. He then asked the audience to pray with him that nobody would leave his lectures being impressed with John Powell but would instead be impressed with who they are.

Sadly, Fr. Powell was later disgraced for sexual misconduct with female college students. One wonders if he was able to keep his footing in light of his huge popularity, or if he failed to take his own advice and fell in love with his press clippings.

Abraham Lincoln said that anybody can handle adversity. If you want to test a person's character, give him or her power. Being a best-selling author and popular lecturer gives a person a lot of power.

People are always trying to glorify themselves. It's doubly hard to keep our feet on the ground when the world is glorifying us. The singer James Taylor said that he has known very few people who could handle being a celebrity. It almost destroyed him.

When I ask myself what is God's will in my life, I believe it's the simple message Fr. Powell received from God: to help people know how good they are. It doesn't take much to achieve that: a warm greeting, a few open-ended questions, and a lively interest in their responses. Bingo, you've made that person's day.

I assume that everyone I encounter is having a bad day. They are feeling like they have nothing to offer to the world. They're feeling marginalized by everything and everyone around them. They need to know that they matter, that they belong.

Ellwood Dowd in *Harvey* encounters an old man whose job is to move a lever that opens and closes a gate. Ellwood takes an enthusiastic interest in the man's work. He has him demonstrate what he does and how the mechanical gate works. The man excitedly shows him. Ellwood makes this man feel like he's performing the most interesting and important task in the world. The old man beams with pride. Ellwood has given him a great gift that will stay with the man for a long time.

When people tell me what they do for a living, I like to follow it up with such questions as: "How did you get into your work?" "What do you like most about your work?" "What don't you like about it?" "What are some of the exciting things that have happened to you with your work?"

Fr. Powell writes that the demographics in our lives don't define us. What defines us is how we feel about who we are and what we do. It is our feelings and experiences that make us unique and special. When I explore people's lives with these types of questions, I seek to heighten their awareness of how special they are.

It's somewhat of an art eliciting this type of information from people. When I succeed, I almost always walk away feeling informed and impressed with what I've learned. And I believe the other person is feeling impressed with who they are.

I was at first disappointed when the director of the counseling center where I worked part-time told me that the other therapists at the center viewed me as a nice person. Nice, I thought, that's a lame compliment. That's the Miss Congeniality Award. Isn't anyone impressed with my clinical knowledge and insights? Those are the things I want people to think of when they think of me.

That was then; this is now. Now, smart is good, but nice is better.

Later, I was interviewing for a position with The Detroit Institute for Children. The interview was short, and one question caught me by surprise.

"If I asked people who know you what they think about you, what would they say?"

I smiled at the cleverness of the question and was surprised by the quickness of my response, "I believe they would say that I'm a nice person."

I got the job.

Nice guys finish last. Good. At the end of the day, it's the person in last place who oftentimes steps up to the winner's podium.

I once tried to be real smart and was surprised at where it got me.

As I mentioned earlier in this book, my assignment at the middle school was to improve the academic and behavioral performances of twelve of the most unmotivated, misbehaving, and poorly achieving youngsters.

I put together the CHAMPS program using a mixture of positive peer culture, social and learning skill building, behavior modification, group therapy, and any other clinical trick I could pull out of my hat to get them to attend classes and stay focused.

I considered CHAMPS a success, with most of its members showing improvements in their school behavior and performance.

But alas, the school principal had other intentions for using the money that funded CHAMPS, and the program was terminated after one year.

At one of the last CHAMPS meetings, I asked the group which one of all the things in the program worked the best in motivating them.

They answered immediately and almost in unison, "You, Mr. Alff."

"Me," I responded in confusion, "what did I have to do with it?"

"We didn't want to disappoint you," they said.

Here I had spent the whole school year racking my clinical brain for techniques that would motivate these youngsters, but in the end, they wanted to succeed because they knew that I liked them, and they in turn liked me.

I recalled something one of the CHAMPS said to me, months before. He told me that he had had a lot of counselors over the years, and he could tell that it was only a job for them. "But you're different, Mr. Alff," he said, "I can tell you really like us."

Another time, a teacher reported to me that one of my CHAMPS had misbehaved in her class. The student implored her not to tell me. It seemed he didn't want to disappoint me.

Sister Helen Dorothy! Just saying the name warms my heart.

She was a Gray Nun and my seventh grade teacher at St. Rose of Lima elementary in Buffalo. I was a bundle of social insecurities and academic failures. She entrusted me with tasks I didn't think I could do. I did them, and with each success, my self-confidence grew. I left that school year with a kernel of self-confidence that grew in fits and starts all through my life.

Sister Helen Dorothy. God bless you, wherever you are.

My friend Dick was captain and a star player for the Detroit Junior Red Wings hockey team when he was a young man. A few years ago, he ran into the son of the team's trainer. This person said that what he remembered most about Dick was how really nice he was toward everyone.

It wasn't Dick's considerable hockey-playing skills that left the lasting impression on him; it was his niceness.

Howard is a friend of mine who struggled through the aftermath of a failed marriage and the need to rebuild his career as a lawyer. During this difficult period in his life, he invited me to participate in a bible study he was conducting at his home. I went and was struck by the strange assortment of people there – including an unemployed gay chef, a young man with cerebral palsy who struggled to walk and who slurred all of his words, a woman with a history of schizophrenia, and various other lost souls.

Howard made all of them feel welcomed, wanted and important.

It was a holy place.

When I start therapy with anyone, my first priority is always to build a positive relationship with that person. If that's in place, anything I do afterward will probably work.

That has always been my strength as a therapist; I like people. In some ways, I'm like the American humorist Will Rogers, who said he never met a person he didn't like.

But then, I don't think I could have put together the bible study group Howard did. The Howards of the world are very special people. They light the way for the rest of us.

In my years with The Wellness Plan, I was most proud of the Rx Caring program.

I was given the assignment to implement a program that would improve staff-patient relations. I assembled the Rx Caring program. It involved eleven training sessions that used a variety of teaching techniques that demonstrated to the staff how to effectively interact with plan members. These patient relationship skills were basically common sense and common courtesy, yet they were all too often not practiced. They included such practices as addressing the patient by his or her name, identifying yourself, keeping the waiting patient informed, explaining what you're doing and why, and educating the patient.

I continuously reminded the staff that the whole Rx Caring program could be summed up as follows: Never, never ignore people. Always pay attention to the patients.

It doesn't take much to do that. Focus on them for a few minutes, listen to what they have to say, and acknowledge how they see the world.

The Rx Caring program was successful in that patient complaints and plan dropouts showed a significant decline. Though these components weren't studied, I'm confident that treatment compliance and health status also increased for plan members.

"Nice" works.

I don't have to agree with someone to acknowledge how he or she sees the world. You like to gamble; tell me about the excitement it brings you. Your parents demand that you be in by eleven o'clock at night? What a bummer! Tell me why you're a Republican, a Democrat, a Libertarian. I want to know and learn.

I must first live in your house for a while before I can begin to suggest ways of rearranging the furniture.

For over two decades, I volunteered at a Detroit soup kitchen two or three times a year. I liked working at the front door, where I controlled the flow of the patrons. This task allowed me to interact with them. They appreciated the food they received, but I think they appreciated even more the warm welcome and brief conversations I tried to have with each one of them. I would thank them for their patience, kibitz with them, and tell them to have a good week, always with very positive body language.

This was my way of acknowledging and affirming them. It may have been the only affirmation they received that week.

As was noted earlier, most people move back and forth between the room labeled "hell" where self-glorification, self-righteousness, self-justification, blaming, faultfinding, and scapegoating reign, and the room labeled "heaven" where people spend their time recognizing, encouraging, and affirming others.

Almost everyone knows, or at least senses, these two approaches to living, and even though they frequently succumb to the self-centered life style, they strive to live a life that nourishes others.

There are some individuals who see only one approach to living, which is self-glorification. They either have no idea that there is another way to live or have no desire to live it.

The search for how to live a more fulfilled life now takes us to a place most people would rather not go, but one that nonetheless must be examined in order to find and defeat the sneaky and pernicious enemy to human happiness and purpose. It's the realm of evil.

MAN AGAINST EVIL

Or, It ain't always the other guy.

The Lord was angry at what David had done, and he sent Nathan the prophet to tell this story to David:

A rich man and a poor man lived in the same town. The rich man owned a lot of sheep and cattle, but the poor man had only one little lamb that he had bought and raised. The lamb became a pet for him and his children. He even let it eat from his plate and drink from his cup and sleep on his lap. The lamb was like one of his own children.

One day someone came to visit the rich man, but the rich man didn't want to kill any of his own sheep or cattle and serve it to the visitor. So he stole the poor man's little lamb and served it instead.

David was furious with the rich man and said to Nathan, "I swear by the living Lord that the man who did this deserves to die! And because he didn't have any pity on the poor man, he will have to pay four times what the lamb was worth."

Then Nathan told David:"*You are that rich man! ...You murdered Uriah the Hittite* by having the Ammonites kill him, so you could take his wife."

2 Samuel 12:1-7,9

Deliver us from evil.
From the Lord's Prayer

Like most kids my age in elementary school, I delighted in riding my bike, going to the local swimming pool in the summer, and playing cards with my brothers and sisters. That's most kids. There was one kid on the block who delighted in something else.

One afternoon, this kid led a few of us down into his basement. He brought out a jar of live bugs and insects. He excitedly took individual bugs and insects out of the jar, pinned them to a surface, and beamed a hot light on them. We watched as they slowly burned and died.

I didn't understand what the "fun" was, but the kid focusing the light was certainly enjoying himself.

Another incident that I remember of cruelty to animals occurred a few years later. I was with a group of youngsters at a riverbank in Buffalo. The kids tossed food that floated on the water and then merrily pelted the gulls with stones and rocks as the birds descended to scoop up the food.

I can't remember if I joined in the "fun."

I learned years later that the boy who enjoyed burning small creatures to death became a Jesuit priest. I wonder if that decision was in part an act of expiation.

As a freshman in Catholic high school, I learned there was a tradition that during the first week of school upperclassmen could collar incoming freshmen, and they had to do whatever the upperclassman ordered them to do.

I didn't think the practice would affect me, but it did.

An upperclassman stopped me on the street. He dropped a coin on the pavement and ordered me to push it forward with my nose.

I got down on my hands and knees and struggled to move the coin with my nose as he stood over me. People passing in cars must have witnessed this strange scene. Only after I had reached the goal did he release me.

He had power over me and used it to subjugate and humiliate me. Years later, after entering the workaday world, I began to understand the close relationship between power and evil.

My friend Bob and I were in early high school, and we made money during the summer caddying at Buffalo area country clubs. On this particular morning, we went to our usual country club to caddy but found no work there. We decided to hitchhike to another country club that we had never been to and to try our luck there.

We arrived there, walked to the caddy shack, sat down, and waited for an assignment. The room was crowded with other hopeful caddies, who soon began to shoot angry looks at Bob and me. We were obviously not welcome, so we got up to leave.

We started walking down the road to the highway outside of the club. Many of the other caddies also got up and followed us. Soon, Bob and I were being pushed, shoved, and spat upon by the caddies behind us. The smaller caddies sprinted in front of us and tried to trip us. Stones and other debris that lay on or near the road were hurled at us. Things were starting to look grim. Bob and I were about to break into a run when we saw a worker astride a utility pole at the entrance of the country club. He was observing the whole scene. The crowd behind us also must have seen him as they stopped their harassment, turned and walked away. The man on the pole smiled and waved to us.

Marge and I have friends who live alongside that country club. I have often sat on their deck, enjoying a morning cup of tea and the peaceful vista. As beautiful as the setting is, I still think about the scare I had there many decades before.

I was a Boy Scout in the fifth or sixth grade. Part of the Scout program was for a den of younger Scouts to periodically go to an older Scout's home on a Saturday afternoon, where the senior Scout made a presentation on some aspect of scouting. That day, the senior Scout made a thorough and very interesting presentation on snakes.

We were having snacks afterward when the presenter's father invited us to see something. He told us he was a detective for the Buffalo Police Department and showed us a room housing articles from many crimes he had investigated throughout his career. The objects ranged from the commonplace to the bizarre, including guns, knives, ropes, blunt objects, and most fascinating, jars containing fingers and hands floating in preserving fluid. Each object had a tag that connected it to a particular crime.

The father explained to us the relationship between the object, the crime, and his investigation. He was very proud of his record in solving these crimes.

I felt that I was being led through a macabre museum of evil by an avenging human angel. His message was, "Evil will not go unpunished in Buffalo as long as I'm around."

It was the summer of my sophomore year of college, and I was hitchhiking from Buffalo to Salt Lake City to visit one of my sisters who was doing Catholic missionary work there. I was to meet her and then travel with her and members of her group to see sites in the American Southwest.

I was about a half day from my destination in Salt Lake City when a station wagon pulled up. I got in. Two men in their early twenties occupied it; one was driving, and the other was in the front passenger seat. We began to talk, and they announced that they were low on money. They spoke about going to an Army recruiting station where they would receive a cash bonus for enlisting. My gut told me that I was in danger being in the car and that I should exit it pronto.

I failed to do that. Instead, I fell asleep in the back seat. I awoke in the middle of the night. The car was pulled over on the side of a desolate road, and the driver was sleeping in the front seat and his buddy was asleep in the back.

They soon awoke as the sun came up. The fellow in the back returned to the front seat, and the driver resumed driving. Suddenly, the driver pulled over to the side of the road. It was another desolate spot, with not a person, structure, or even a car in sight.

The driver said that he was still sleepy and wanted to sleep some more. He told his buddy to get into the back of the station wagon. The buddy said he didn't want to. The driver persisted, and the buddy resisted.

As I sat behind them it was apparent to me that the driver was telling his buddy to get behind me so that the two of them could jump, rob, and possibly kill me. They could easily dispose of my body in the desolate surroundings. No one would find me.

It seemed my life hung in the balance. There was little I could do to change things.

The buddy won out. The driver started the engine and drove on.

I worked hard to make friendly conversation after that, and even bought them breakfast in Salt Lake City when we got there.

My life was spared on the frightening morning on a very lonesome road in remote Utah.

When a Wellness Plan member was referred to its Social and Mental Health Services Department for psychiatric treatment, the procedure was for one of the staff social workers to conduct a psychosocial intake assessment, followed by the development and implementation of a treatment plan. This plan usually called for the patient to see the staff psychiatrist for psychotropic medications and one of the staff social workers for psychiatric counseling.

As I noted earlier, the new staff psychiatrist was feeling overwhelmed by the number of patients he was treating, and he told me not to refer any more new patients to him for a while. I should instead persuade new patients to undergo psychiatric counseling to the exclusion of psychotropic medications for at least a short time.

A young African American male was referred for psychiatric treatment, and I did the intake assessment. I can't recall if I felt he needed to see the psychiatrist for medications or not, but the words of the psychiatrist rang in my ears, and I set out to convince him to see me for counseling instead of seeing the psychiatrist for medications.

He wasn't buying it. I softened it by telling him that if a few sessions of counseling failed to help him, I would then refer him to the psychiatrist. He continued to insist that he wanted see the psychiatrist while I continued to insist that counseling was the best choice for him.

Suddenly, his whole demeanor changed, and with it the whole atmosphere in the room. He shot a look at me that chilled me to the marrow. He didn't raise his voice or become overtly belligerent; he just changed. There was something in the tone of his voice and the look in his eyes that said that if I continued to obstruct his desires, he would seriously hurt me. He was no longer the same person. He was an instrument of a very malignant force. I knew I was in imminent danger.

I have worked for over thirty years with patients who harbored bizarre delusions, heard non-existent voices, and were walking time bombs, but I never felt imperiled in their presence. For the first time in my career, I was genuinely scared.

I quickly backtracked. I told him that he was right; he should see the psychiatrist, and I would make the referral immediately.

That about-face didn't immediately defuse the situation. He continued to look at me in a very menacing way. I continued to assure him that his wishes would be met. Slowly, his demeanor softened, and I could feel the danger pass.

Again, the cold winds of evil had blown into my life, and once again, I had escaped.

I had, over my years at The Wellness Plan, made a number of home visits. Some of these visits were in scary neighborhoods where I needed to be very careful. I never encountered a problem. On one occasion, I went to see a client in one of the city's housing projects. I entered the lobby of the high-rise building and pressed the elevator button. I was suddenly gripped by an overwhelming fear. I had no reason to be fearful, as I saw no one around me. I nevertheless sensed impending disaster, the way certain land animals will know that a tsunami is heading to shore before there is any physical evidence of it. I immediately left the building and returned to the office.

Did I experience a panic attack or an evil presence? I don't think it was the former, as I have never had a panic attack before or after that experience in my life. I believe something very dangerous was closing in on me.

Maurice was a very handsome, four-year-old African American boy in one of the Head Start programs where I was the mental health consultant. His verbal skills were advanced for his age. He was evidently very intelligent, even precocious.

There was also something very different, even peculiar, about him. He was always doing hurtful things to the other children, but it wasn't because of the usual reasons, such as poor impulse control, intermittent explosive disorder, or lack of social skill development. These were conditions that could be addressed and corrected. There was something cunning and very malicious about Maurice's behavior.

He always denied his wrongdoings, which isn't uncommon for children of this age, but he would skillfully try to shift the blame on to the other children. When he couldn't escape responsibility, he would change tactics by asking for a hug. Even his hugs were frightening. They weren't tender hugs; his squeeze was aggressive and even painful at times.

He told one of his teachers that he didn't like the baby she was carrying. Once, when her head was turned, he attempted to hit her in the stomach.

His teachers and I met with Maurice's parents to share our concerns and to seek their cooperation to help him. They refused to hear us. They wouldn't believe that Maurice could do anything wrong and instead found fault with his teachers and his fellow students for the problems attributed to their son. Nothing was done to help Maurice.

Years later, Maurice's teachers and I would occasionally wonder what became of him. We always feared the worst.

Marsha looked as depressed an individual as I ever encountered in my office. She sat slouched in the seat with her eyes glued to the floor as she mumbled her words. I asked her about her mood and stressors and received incoherent responses. I finally told her that I was going to arrange for her to be admitted to a psychiatric hospital.

Suddenly, her head popped up, her body straightened, and she said in a lively voice, "Do you know what she did last night? She went for the knives. We fought over them until I finally got them away from her.

"I'm so sick of her constant smoking. And God, is that apartment gloomy. I keep telling her to pull up the shades and open the windows. Get some light and fresh air into the place.

"She needs to get out, go dancing, meet new people."

As I slowly recovered from the shock at seeing this transformation and suspecting a multiple personality, I hesitantly said, "Who are you?"

"I'm Joyce. I'm her, but then, I'm not her."

This started a fairly long clinical experience with a woman who straddled the fence between the forces of life and death. Life finally won out, but death was always in the wings, eager to take center stage.

Mary was a wonderful person who I counseled at The Wellness Plan. Her heart was full of love and compassion, as when she picked up stray animals and fought for the rights of unborn children. She also had her demons.

Her childhood on a farm in rural Iowa had frightening and confusing periods where she witnessed the wild mood swings and irrational behavior of her mother who suffered from a manic-depression disorder. She fled this home life only to fall into the hands of a man who sexually exploited her. He once got her to entice one of her sisters to participate in his sexual perversions.

She never forgave herself for doing that. She couldn't shake the belief that she had committed an unforgivable sin.

She saw, to my mind, an opportunity to redress this wrong when her mentally handicapped sister back in Iowa informed her that she had had sexual relations with a male acquaintance. Mary believed it was a case of rape and may have convinced her mentally deficient sister of this.

Mary had the resources that played a part in this man's conviction for rape. He was sent to prison.

Mary wasn't finished with him. She made sure his name was placed on a sexual offenders list, insuring that he would spend the rest of his life living with the consequences of his actions.

Was Mary redressing a terrible wrong that had happened to her sister or was she seeking absolution for her "unforgivable sin?" I don't know.

If it was the latter, then it was a case of a very good person seeking to do a good thing and ending up destroying another human being.

This, I believe, is the subtlest form of evil. Good people doing bad things in the name of good causes.

Zealots for any cause can easily cross this line.

I worked with Paul's wife at the Head Start program. She kept me informed of the hell Paul was being put through at work.

Paul was an automotive engineer who worked with auto suppliers in product development. He impressed me as a hardworking "car guy" who was very intelligent and knew his field of expertise.

His boss at his new job thought differently. He was on Paul's case from the start of his employment there. Nothing Paul did satisfied his boss. His boss micromanaged him and had Paul record his every move during the workday. He kept hinting that if Paul's performance didn't improve, he would lose his job. Paul thought he hated him.

Paul became increasingly unraveled under this onslaught. He became more and more anxious, depressed and irritable at home. He finally quit.

But his boss wasn't finished with Paul. In order for him to receive a severance package from the company, he insisted that Paul sign an agreement stating that he would not work for a competitor for the next five years. This would have effectively ended Paul's professional career.

(Interestingly, Paul's boss constantly accused Paul of incompetence, yet he was fearful that Paul would work for a competitor.)

Paul refused, and left the company without severance pay.

He thought he was finally free of this tyrant. He wasn't.

A competing company quickly hired Paul. Paul's former employer threatened his new company with a lawsuit if they didn't fire Paul. They refused. Nothing came of it. Paul has been happily working for the new company for years.

The emotional scars from that experience have not left Paul. His mood always sours when he thinks of how his former boss treated him.

Paul has since gotten to know the person who succeeded him at his old company. The same ill treatment happened to him. He also quit. They occasionally talk with each other, and this benefits both of them.

My guess is that Paul's abusive boss probably justified his behavior as being good for the company, and possibly Paul.

Power combined with self-righteousness and a "noble cause" is a prescription for a lot of human misery.

Dr. R, M.D. cut an impressive figure, particularly to the graduate social work and psychology students who were working with him for the summer at the mental health clinic.

I think he was a professor at the local university department of psychiatry, and the students at the center assumed that he had a successful private practice.

And why not? An aura of professional fitness surrounded him.

He was also very cool. He drove a muscular motorcycle; his image complete with a black leather jacket, white helmet, and shades.

As supervising psychiatrist for the clinic, it was his responsibility to insure that the people who used the crisis phone service and who came to the center for short-term counseling received competent services. He sought to achieve this objective by critiquing cases presented to him either individually or in a group of staff and student therapists.

Oh yes, there was one other thing about Dr. R: he was one mean son-of-a-bitch.

He wasn't mean in the usual sense of the word. He didn't bark at people, call them names, or threaten them with dismissal. His meanness was much more subtle and pernicious than that. He destroyed their self-confidence.

I first noticed his handiwork when I saw a graduate psychology student leaving his office after what I assumed was a consultation session with him. The student looked scared. He was so frightened he could hardly walk.

I wondered what had happened to him.

I soon found out.

Weekly case conference meetings at the center were opportunities for the therapists to receive feedback from fellow staff members on how to improve the work they were doing with clients. The format for the meeting consisted of a therapist presenting the details of a case, followed by questions, comments, and suggestions from the other therapists on ways to improve the clinical experience. It was usually pretty benign stuff.

This student's presentation and subsequent discussion was proceeding normally when Dr. R began to grill her on the justification for her psychiatric diagnosis, and the rationale for her treatment plan and interventions.

Her answers didn't satisfy Dr. R.

With a look of grave concern on his face, he proceeded to lecture the student and the rest of us on how imperative it was for therapists to make an accurate diagnosis and to know exactly what they were doing before probing into the tricky recesses of a client's subconscious mind. He drew a parallel to surgery. Woe to the surgeon who removes a patient's liver when the problem is the pancreas. He punctuated his observation by dramatically running his hand down the center of his chest to simulate the opening of the thoracic cavity. In other words, woe to the psychotherapist who dredges up long-repressed materials from a person's subconscious mind and then mishandles them.

The message was clear. This student therapist didn't know what she was doing, and in her well-intended but misguided way, she was doing irreparable harm to this poor patient. The patient and student were doomed. The patient would probably never recover from her malpractice, and the student would have to spend the rest of her life knowing the damage she had caused.

It was all very dramatic, and it scared the daylights out of every student in the room, including me. I thought about the clients I was seeing. I could only imagine the damage I was doing to their fragile psyches. What if they failed to keep their next appointment? I wouldn't have an opportunity to repair the damage I had done. If they failed to keep their appointments, I was sure that it was because they had either collapsed into a heap of emotional wreckage that required psychiatric hospitalization or had committed suicide.

Dr. R brought the session to a close by gravely instructing the student on how best to put Humpty-Dumpty back together again.

As I stepped away from this frightful scene, I began to mull over Dr. R's contention that psychiatric counseling is akin to surgery. To a psychoanalyst, the unconscious mind might be a labyrinth that must be carefully navigated, but the therapists at the center were simply trying to help clients explore emotionally difficult experiences in their lives that might be interfering with their ability to function effectively in the present. It wasn't brain surgery. Besides, if talking about certain experiences was too emotionally upsetting for a client, he or she could simply use a few defense mechanisms, such as denial or rationalization, to silence uncomfortable thoughts and feelings.

I reasoned that only good could come out of these sessions, not the emotional ruin Dr. R was predicting.

As my anxiety waned, my anger toward Dr. R waxed.

It was my turn to present a case at the next conference. I did so and awaited comments. Dr. R soon entered in with the expected questions on what I based my diagnosis on and what I hoped to achieve with my intervention techniques. He challenged my responses.

Unlike the previous students who were subject to his harsh scrutiny, I didn't recoil. I defended what I was doing, if only for the sake of doing battle with him.

He acted like I was just an annoying fly. "Mr. Alff," he finally said, "I would never take you on as a student because your thinking is too linear." Translated: "Mr. Alff, you're too dumb to understand and appreciate the complexities of the human mind and how to treat its disorders."

I recall we just glared at each other. I should have said to him, "Well, Dr. R, if I needed to see a psychiatrist, I would never go to you because you hate people. I may be a simple thinker, but you're a son-of-a-bitch."

I might have gone one round with Dr. R, but if I had been a permanent staff member there, I'm sure he would have gotten rid of me. Evil people don't like annoying flies buzzing around them.

Alfred Hitchcock movies will always frighten us. They are about ordinary people, living ordinary lives in ordinary settings when something very unordinary happens. That something is evil.

Sara and Dan were ordinary people. Sara was a caring elementary school teacher, and Dan was a quiet, hard-working guy. Their marriage of one year was ordinary and happy. Things then began to change.

Sara knew Dan was close to his mother but didn't realize how close until after they married. His mother came to their house daily to do laundry, clean, and prepare meals. Sara tolerated it for a while but then gently urged her not to be "so helpful." Dan's mother complained to her son about Sara's ingratitude. Dan supported his mother.

Dan began to drink alcohol more and was striking Sara when inebriated. Sara at first attributed his abusive behavior to work stress. They came to me for counseling. They agreed that his drinking was the problem and that he would stop hitting her if he stopped drinking. I believed Dan harbored subconscious anger toward his mother and was displacing it onto Sara. I was certain that the beatings would continue, with or without Dan's drinking. I advised Sara to give Dan an ultimatum: "Hit me one more time and I will leave you." They stopped coming to therapy. I called Sara and tried to impress on her the seriousness of her situation. Sara believed that patience and love would improve Dan. I again told her what she must do if Dan hit her again. She believed things were returning to normal while I seriously doubted it.

Nothing returns to normal when evil enters our lives. Life gets worse, most times a lot worse.

Sara was trapped in a dehumanizing and very dangerous marriage. Some people are trapped in evil cults. It can easily happen: Catch a person at a vulnerable stage in their life; "love-bomb" them; confuse their thinking; cut them off from their family, friends, and other supports; and make them reliant on The Leader who seems to possess special qualities. If he tells you to drink the Kool-Aid, you unquestioningly drink it.

The American Heritage Dictionary defines evil as "causing ruin, injury, or pain; harmful." What distinguishes cruelty and meanness from evil? When does a bad person, or worse yet, a good person become an evil person?

M. Scott Peck, M.D. is a psychiatrist and best-selling author of the books, *The Road Less Traveled* and *People of the Lie*. He writes that, "It is not their sin *per se* that characterizes evil people, rather it is the subtlety and persistence and consistency of their sins. This is because the central defect of the evil is not the sin but the refusal to acknowledge it"(Peck in Zweig and Abrams, eds. p. 176).

"They (evil people) are characterized by the *absolute* refusal to tolerate the sense of their sinfulness."

He continues, "A predominant characteristic, however, of the behavior of those I call evil is scapegoating. Because in their hearts they consider themselves above reproach, they must lash out at anyone who does reproach them. They sacrifice others to preserve their self-image of perfection ... (They) attack others instead of facing their own failures" (Ibid. p. 178).

Dr. Peck further states, (evil people) "are utterly dedicated to preserving their self-image of perfection, they are unceasingly engaged in the effort to maintain the appearance of moral purity" (Ibid. p. 179).

"They cannot or will not tolerate the pain of self-reproach ... Evil originates not in the absence of guilt but in the effort to escape it." (Ibid. p. 180)

Even more chilling is his observation that, "Evil people may be rich or poor, educated or uneducated. There is little that is dramatic about them. They are not designated criminals. More often than not they will be 'solid citizens'—Sunday school teachers, policemen, or bankers, and active in the PTA" (Ibid. p. 176).

They are people who subtly, persistently, and consistently defend, glorify, and justify themselves and in the process blame, scapegoat, and harm people around them. They have no conscious sense that they are anything but wonderful and honorable people.

Dr. Peck comments that these people do not show up on the psychiatrist's couch. "The submission to the discipline of self-observation required by the psychoanalysis does, in fact, seem to them like suicide. The most significant reason we know so little scientifically about human evil is simply that the evil are so extremely reluctant to be studied" (Ibid. p. 180).

Evil people, according to Dr. Peck's definition, are quantitatively, not qualitatively, different from other people. All humans are prone to self-glorifying and blaming behavior, and practice them to varying degrees and for varying durations. They will, however, often question and seek to at least alter their self-centered behavior. Evil people have no such qualms or scruples. They delight in self-glorification and will not only blame others when their self-centered plans are thwarted; they will destroy them. They soon begin to destroy people even when they present no overt threat to them. Evil people are very suspicious. Their swath of destruction grows larger and larger until it curves back and destroys them.

BEWARE: Evil people can be extremely charming, seductive and persuasive. They totally believe in themselves, and this confidence can be very attractive, particularly to women. They are master manipulators who know how to play on people's emotions. They will weave a web of glamorous achievements, grandiose plans, and importance, which is so convincing because they actually believe these falsehoods themselves. When people, particularly women, begin to question their claims, they turn on them, often with deadly results. They display no regret or remorse for their actions because he or she "had it coming."

There is no question that there are evil people in the world. But is there a cosmic evil presence?

There are numerous personal accounts by people who believe that they were protected or guided through harrowing times by a beneficent force. I relate two such personal experiences in the next chapter of this book. Is there, conversely, a malignant force in the world that is intent on human discord and destruction? A force that is commonly attributed to Satan or the devil? (As the comedian Flip Wilson frequently said, "The devil made me do it.")

I enjoyed, as a youngster, watching the half hour dramas on television. One I remember featured a traveler who was caught in a storm and found his way to a monastery where he spent the night. He heard a man screaming from within the monastery. The monks explained that the screaming man was the devil, whom they had captured years before and held captive. The monks pointed to the peace and prosperity that the world had been experiencing since the man was held in captivity as proof that their prisoner was the devil. They told the traveler to ignore the screaming and not to go near the cell.

The screaming continued into the night, and the traveler made his way to its source. The man in the cell pleaded to the traveler to release him. He said the monks were crazy and that his only crime was kissing a girl.

The traveler didn't know who to believe, the monks or the prisoner. He decided to remove the bar from the door that allowed the prisoner to leave the cell. As the prisoner left, the earth shook and he changed into a grotesque creature.

Decades ago, while in the Army, a few of the soldiers and I went to the base movie theatre and saw the then very popular movie, *Rosemary's Baby,* starring Mia Farrow. It's a frightening movie that presents the Christian Nativity with a twist: the devil is incarnate rather than the Son of God.

In our discussion of the movie afterwards, one of the soldiers offered this insightful comment, "If the good guys can do it, then the bad guys can also do it."

I took that to mean that just as there are good forces in the world, there are also bad forces. If God is involved in human affairs, so is the devil.

I can't remember what prompted Dr. Steinberg to ask the surprising question to the Abnormal Psychology class of about thirty students. "Who believes in the devil?" he asked. Two hands went into the air, mine and another student's. I felt embarrassed and slightly stupid, as the other students who didn't raise their hands looked at the two of us as if we were holdovers from the Dark Ages.

How should a person respond when they believe they are in the presence of evil?

In Army basic training at Ft. Dix, NJ, there was an African American soldier in the unit who was mentally slow and goofy. Some of the other soldiers made fun of him. One day, a group of them assembled around Claude to harass him. I stepped forward and told them to lay off him. One of the harassers turned to me and said, "You're not big enough to talk like that." I backed off.

Joseph Stalin, the evil premier of communist Russia, was once discussing an international situation Russia was involved in when the Pope was mentioned. Stalin dismissed the Pontiff with the comment, "How many battalions does he command?"

It's probably the most audience pleasing movie scenario going: An evil person or group comes into town, intimidates everyone, and does a lot of damage before someone steps up—say, Charles Bronson,

Batman, the Spiderman—and kicks the tar out of the malefactor(s). The audience breaks out in cheers.

That might work in the movies, but real life is another matter.

Martin Luther King, Jr. and Mahatma Gandhi conquered evil by sacrificing themselves to it so that the world could see racism and colonialism in all of its horrible ugliness. Jesus allowed evil to have its way on Golgotha, only to defeat it three days later with His resurrection. Good Friday becomes Easter Sunday!

There's a gripping scene in the movie, *Gandhi* that displays the courage it takes to unmask and eventually conquer evil. Gandhi and his followers are ordered by the British commander not to cross a line. British soldiers stand ready to punish anyone who disobeys the command. Gandhi steps over the line. He's clubbed by a British soldier and dragged away. The next Indian in line steps over the line. He is clubbed by a British soldier and dragged away. The next courageous Indian, and then another, and then another do the same thing. The sickening brutality continues until every Gandhi follower is left bloodied and removed.

Episodes like that broke the back of British colonialism in India.

Martin Luther King, Jr. and his followers stood up to fire hoses, clubs, attack dogs, prison cells, threats to their families, and finally death to break the back of Jim Crow racism in America.

I briefly stood up for Claude that day, but how many times have I allowed racist comments to pass in conversations for fear of being rejected?

I like to say nice things about Detroit and its residents. At gatherings when suburban Detroiters are saying derogatory things about Detroit, and by inference its predominantly African American residents, everyone is usually nodding their heads in agreement. When I try to shift the conversation to positive things about Detroit, I'm looked at like I just spilled mustard on everyone.

People like to think that evil is about good guys versus bad guys, and they are always on the side of the good guys. Think again.

I believe that there is a way to determine if a person is prone to becoming an evildoer. If a person states that he or she would never engage in evil behavior, look out. Those people, I believe, are susceptible to performing evil things.

If I was an impressionable youth, which I was, and raised in an anti-Semitic German home during the rise of the Third Reich, I probably would have been goose-stepping with the rest of the nation. I frequently remind myself of that sobering fact. I do it to guard against falling into the clutches of evil.

To be forewarned is to be forearmed.

Evil behavior usually starts with small, seemingly innocuous behavior that insidiously grows and wraps its malignant tentacles around us.

The *Wall Street Journal* once had an op-ed piece that went something like this:

"Several years ago, I was made building inspector for my town. When I took the job, I was aware of the corrupt reputation that went along with this job, and I was thoroughly committed to being honest. A few days before Christmas, a box arrived that was sent by a local builder. Inside was an expensive ham. I immediately instructed my secretary to return it. However, the company that sold the ham said they couldn't accept the return of perishable goods. So I decided to donate the ham to a local shelter.

We did this for a few years, until one year when the ham came on Christmas Eve. The shelters by this time were fully stocked. I thought to myself, *Well, this food shouldn't go to waste*, so I took it home. The next year, I did the same, and so on, until my last year in this job, when I sat back and wondered to myself, *Where is my Christmas ham from that builder?*"

Conquering evil often takes something bigger than what humans possess.

At the end of Catholic masses decades ago, the priest would kneel at the foot of the altar and together with the congregants implore saints to provide them protection, with the congregants reciting, "Pray for us." The litany always ended with the prayer, "Save the world, save Russia."

Decades later, the evils of communism ended with the fall of the Berlin Wall. People behind the Iron Curtain were at last free.

Historians have ascribed a variety of reasons for the collapse of communism, particularly the policies of President Ronald Reagan. I doubt if any of those historians reported on the millions of Catholic churchgoers who prayed for the deliverance of Russia.

In the movie, *Harvey*, Elwood is explaining who Harvey is. He says that in a bar everyone has big dreams and big problems. He then introduces them to Harvey, who is bigger than all of their dreams and problems. They leave impressed.

There are some things in human experience that are so big, so magnificent, and so unquestionably powerful that all we can do is gasp in awe when we consider the glory of God's creation. His power trumps all other power.

Marge and I recently visited a number of national parks in the American Southwest, including the Grand Canyon. Each time I gazed into its multicolored canyons, I was left speechless. Its grandeur, majesty, and beauty overpowered me. I felt wonderfully insignificant in its presence.

Tourists were snapping pictures by the thousands with the expectation of capturing those qualities. It can't be done. In fact, even words like grandeur, majesty and beauty fail to do it justice. These natural wonders are meant to humble us in a wonderful way.

"Be still and know that I am God..." (Psalm 46:10)

If God is bigger than evil and in a position to defeat it, why don't humans turn to Him for help? It would be so easy. Yet we don't.

Why not?

Our journey now takes us to one of the most perplexing issues humans struggle with: our relationship with our Creator.

MAN AGAINST GOD

Or, Your arm's too short to box with God.

The Lord responding to Job's complaints that he's being ill-treated.

Then the Lord answered Job out of the whirlwind:
"Who is this that darkens counsel by words without knowledge. . .
Where were you when I laid the foundation of the earth?
Tell me, if you have understanding.
Who determined its measurements—surely you know!
   or who stretched the line upon it?
On what were its bases sunk,
   Or who laid its cornerstone,
when the morning stars sang together. . .
Or who shut in the sea with the doors. . .
 and prescribed bounds for it. . .
And the Lord said to Job:

"Shall a faultfinder contend with the Almighty...
Have you an arm like God.
 and can you thunder with a voice like his?"
 Job 38-40

Now the serpent was more subtle than any other wild creature that the Lord God had made. He said to the woman, "Did God say, 'You shall not eat of any tree of the garden?'" And the woman said to the serpent, "We may eat of the fruit of the trees of the garden; but God said, 'You shall not eat of the fruit of the tree which is in the midst of the garden, neither shall you touch it, lest you die.'" But the serpent said to the woman, "**You will not die.** For God knows that when you eat of it your eyes will be opened, and **you will be like God**, knowing good and evil." So when the woman saw that the tree was good for food, and that it was a delight to the eyes, and that the tree was to be desired to make one wise, she took of its fruit and ate; and she also gave some to her husband, and he ate."
 Genesis 3: 1-7

My father, Herbert Alff, was full of aphorisms. He would say, for instance, "If I'm not canonized a saint after I die, there's been a serious miscarriage of justice."

Another one I remember was: "If you want to make money in America, start a religion." He might have added: "And tell everyone in that religion that they can be just like God."

What could be more natural? People naturally seek immortality through self-glorification, so turn that drive into a religion. The gospel is simple: We all possess an underlying divinity; believe it and it's yours. Bingo! You're God. Double Bingo! The church is full to the rafters and the money is pouring in.

Dad was certainly ahead of his time in his thinking, though I'm thankful he stuck to selling paper and other more useful products.

If people gave this notion of becoming God any serious thought, I doubt they would want the job. It's a ton of problems with barely a word of thanks. Besides, it can't be done. There's a huge gap between the Creator and the created, and that's not about to disappear by believing that it can, and will, happen.

Humans are intent on self-glorification. They want people to pay homage to them. They seek to be all-knowing and all-powerful. They want to sit in judgment on others. They want to be just like God; make that, be God. They don't have time for that guy who created the universe and everything in it. In fact, they would like to get rid of Him and put themselves in His place. Funny thing: They honestly think it can be done.

Fortunately Dad just wanted to be a saint. I don't think he would have made a very good god.

Two Head Start children who I observed were talking about a classmate who had recently died.

"He's in the ground," stated the one child.

"No, he's in heaven," replied the other child.

"No, he's in the ground," insisted the first child.

"No, he's in heaven," insisted the second child.

"He's in the ground."

"He's in heaven."

This dispute has been going on since the dawn of humankind, with about as much resolution as displayed by these four-year-olds. Yet it continues, oftentimes with tragic results.

I was in high school and worked for a summer at a very exclusive club in the Adirondacks in upstate New York. My brother Paul was working at a nearby resort. He had a car and he picked me up one night for dinner. Afterward, he dropped me off at a path that wound through the woods and led to my cabin.

I began walking and soon found myself enveloped in total darkness. I became disoriented and very scared as I struggled to move forward. I considered getting down on my hands and knees and feeling my way along the path. I instead continued to baby step my way along. Suddenly, I glimpsed the faintest light. I was full of joy. I had a bearing. I moved toward the light, and it took me to my cabin.

Being lost, confused, and not knowing where to turn next is very frightening. People in these situations are in trouble and need help. Yet they frequently refuse to admit that they are lost or to seek the help they need. I have been in those situations many times in my life and have received help whether I asked for it or not.

Things couldn't have gotten any worse in my life.

I had recently graduated from college and didn't have the foggiest idea what to do next. The Vietnam War was heating up, and I knew I didn't want any part of that killing machine. I was accepted for Peace Corps training to serve in Turkey for two years but was deemed unqualified at the end of the summer training program in southern California. I returned home to Buffalo resigned to being drafted and probably going to Vietnam.

I decided to salve my bruised feelings from being rejected by the Peace Corps and to temporarily blot out the thoughts of possibly going to Vietnam by spending a few days at my old college town drinking and catching up with old buddies there.

I was knocking down beers at a popular haunt when I struck up a conversation with a stranger. I informed him of my plight.

He advised me to end the agonizing waiting and volunteer for the draft. Don't enlist, he warned, as that would result in a three year military commitment instead of two years, and it wouldn't matter which military specialty I had; the Army would put me in the infantry and ship me off to the rice paddies of Vietnam.

I would undergo a battery of intelligence and achievement tests early on in basic training, he said. He emphasized that I should take them seriously and to do well on them as they would be used to determine my assignment. The combination of my college degree, good test results, and only a two-year obligation should result in fairly comfortable and safe stateside duty.

He sternly warned that while in basic training I would be pressured to enter Officers Candidate School because of my college degree. "Don't do it," he warned, "it's a one-way ticket to Vietnam."

He had given me a roadmap out of my troubles.

I did exactly as he instructed. Everything that he predicted happened: the tests, the pressure to enter OCS, and most important, remaining in the states.

"Never heard of that one before, Alff," said my basic training sergeant when I told him I was assigned to the Kimborough Army Hospital Mental Health Unit at Ft. George G. Meade, Maryland as a mental health technician.

I stayed there for the remainder of my two-year stint.

It was not only very interesting work, but it also showed me how to pursue a career in mental health.

I got an early release from the Army to attend the WSU Social Work Graduate School that was partially paid for by the GI Bill.

I often thought that had I been sent to Turkey as a Peace Corps volunteer as I originally planned, it would have only delayed my being drafted and probably being sent to Vietnam two years later.

Two years earlier, I was sitting at my desk in my college dorm concluding that my dreams of a career in psychology were over. I was now poised to enter the mental health field. It happened because of the advice a stranger gave to me in a noisy college bar.

Who was that person? How did we strike up a conversation? College students were the only ones who frequented that bar. How did he know so much about the Army? Why did I trust him so much that I followed his advice to a T? What amazed me the most was that the plan he laid out for me not only kept me out of Vietnam but also resurrected my dream of a career in the field of mental health.

Who was that person who brought light into my world when everything was so dark?

My favorite reading genre is biographies, followed by histories. People intrigue me. I have read personal accounts of people in dire situations, where their lives hung in the balance. A few have reported a very interesting experience at those moments. As they lay shattered and helpless, a stranger or a voice in their head spoke to them, instructing them on precisely what they must do to survive. Following that advice saved their lives.

An angel? Perhaps.

Sometimes, we're lost and don't realize it. In fact, we couldn't be more confident that we're on the right track. The problem is we're not on the right track. We're happily going in the wrong direction. It's like the lyric from the Simon and Garfunkel song, *Slip Slidin' Away*, "The nearer your destination the more you're slip slidin' away."

I was confident that I was walking toward my goal in life, when in fact I was walking away from it.

I would soon be armed with a M.S.W. degree and would take a position as a child caseworker in Washington, D.C.

A professor at the graduate school told me that the Model Cities Health Program in Detroit was seeking to fill a social worker position and encouraged me to apply for it. I agreed to interview for it, even though I had a job waiting for me in D.C. and had no desire to remain in Detroit. I couldn't have been more relaxed at the interview, seeing that I wasn't interested in the job.

The director of the department and I hit it off immediately as we casually spoke about people we both knew. He then asked me various questions to determine my suitability for the position. He must have liked my answers: He offered me the position then and there. He informed me of the salary, which was twenty-five percent higher than the salary I would have received in D.C. That got my attention. I went home, thought about it, and accepted the position a few days later.

That was easily the best move I've made in my life. The job evolved into a twenty-eight-year career in a health care program that became one of the largest Medicaid HMOs in the country. I served as Director of its Social and Mental Health Services Department during most of that time. The work was both professionally and financially rewarding.

The greatest blessing was the opportunity to continue to date Marge, who was a year behind me in social work school, and to eventually marry her. I'm sure that had I gone to D.C., our relationship would have petered out. It wasn't that serious at the time.

And what a wonderful marriage it has been. We continue to enjoy each other's company. We have raised two great children who are now making wonderful contributions to the world. We are further blessed with a great son- and daughter-in-law, and grandchildren.

In the play, *The Last of Mrs. Lincoln*, a group is commenting on how difficult it must have been for Abe to put up with his wife, Mary Todd Lincoln. Robert, their only surviving child, responded to these comments by saying, "I don't think my father would have been the man he was if not for my mother."

I know that I would not be the person I am today if not for Marge. I owe all the happiness in my life to her.

All of this started with a professor who just happened to think that I would be the right person for a position she knew about. Why did I agree to the interview? What made me take the position when I was set on going to D.C., even if the salary there was lower? Was God looking out for me again?

Ted Turner, the media mogul and billionaire, is reputed to have said that Christianity is for losers. I thought about this comment and concluded that he actually complimented Christians rather than insulted them with his comment.

Evolution doesn't like losers. It tries to get rid of them. It prefers the genes of people like Ted Turner. Ted gets to marry Jane Fonda.

People like Turner's father, who committed suicide, are broken by the world and get left behind. They have lost out in the sweepstakes of life.

The Ted Turners of the world think that these people are weaklings who use religion to compensate for their inadequacies and failures.

Ted Turner is a very smart person, but he's not wise. He doesn't realize that he's as lost and broken as these other people. The difference between him and them is that they acknowledge their need for help and are grateful when they receive it.

Gore Vidal, the well-known author, is reputed to have said that Christianity is a silly religion. Like Ted Turner, he meant to discredit Christianity but instead paid it a compliment. Only a fool would believe the story of Jesus Christ. He was an itinerant rabbi/teacher who roamed the Palestine countryside with a bunch of ill-educated followers. He claimed that he was the Messiah prophesied in the Hebrew covenant with their God. The woods were full at the time with people claiming to be God incarnate, from insane Roman emperors to deluded individuals of every stripe. Jesus picks a fight with the Jewish authorities, and they did what all people in power do when their positions are challenged: they got rid of him.

Jesus' followers regrouped following his death and started a cult by claiming that he rose from the dead, ascended into heaven, and was indeed the Son of God who saved the world from its sins and opened the doors to eternal life.

The whole story sounds cockamamie from start to finish. Only a fool would believe it.

It's a silly story for foolish people.

The Greek playwright Aeschylus said, "It is a profitable thing, if one is wise, to seem foolish."

I've spent my whole life working with losers who needed all the help they could get.

I've worked with clients who were so depressed and anxious that they missed most of the joys in life. One client told me that she and her husband went on a trip, and she spent the whole time worrying about whether she left the toaster on in the kitchen. Some clients couldn't stop thinking or doing silly things, such as touching objects over and over again in the hope of achieving peace of mind. A few unfortunate souls kept hearing voices in their heads that would taunt, insult, or tell them to do foolish and even dangerous things. One person was watching a group of protesters and was convinced that their protest had to do with him, while another believed that TV characters were talking about her. One client lived in fear that an unintended racist tirade would burst forth from his mouth, thereby destroying his professional career. Another client feared the spewing of unintended profanities. There were females who were starving themselves to death or cutting themselves. A whole batch of clients had addictions that they couldn't control, be it to alcohol, drugs, sex, spending, stealing, etc. Many clients were explosive and couldn't stop hurting people they loved.

One of these clients captured her anguish in this way. She said that her mental illness is like being in a house with an intruder who is trying to kill her. The doors and windows are bolted shut, and she can't get out. She's screaming and pounding for help on a picture window at the front of the house. The people who are walking past the house can see her but can't hear her. They think she's crazy. They quicken their pace and move on. She's not only terrified, but she's ostracized from people around her who don't understand what she's going through and won't help her.

She desperately needs someone to say to her, "Tell me what you're going through. I want to understand. I'll try to help you escape your fears."

A funny thing happened on the way to oblivion for a lot of these people who seem to be losers and fools. They found something that is totally off the radar screens for people like Ted Turner and Gore Vidal. They have found the Living God.

Selma taught me this.

Selma wasn't supposed to be full of so much joy and peace. Didn't she know that she was one of the rejects in life? She was an African American woman who lived a lifetime of misfortunes. She was subsisting on Supplemental Disability Benefits and was receiving Medicaid for medical insurance. I was seeing her for counseling to help her cope with the repeated storms in her life.

There was something strangely different about Selma. She wasn't without her emotional difficulties, but she possessed a sense of gratitude and happiness that was out of proportion with her day-to-day problems. She was always thanking Jesus for this, that, and another thing.

I finally said to her, "Selma, why are you always thanking Jesus? You're as poor as a church mouse; you got hit by a car last year; you were left for dead until, as you said, Dr. Jesus took your case; and your children rarely lift a finger to help you."

She didn't hesitate in answering. "Jesus has brought me this far, and he will bring me home."

Selma had a friend, companion, protector, and savior in Jesus, and she rejoiced in that.

Jesus didn't walk by the house when she was screaming at the front window. He walked in and comforted and helped her.

I've encountered numerous clients like Selma, mostly African Americans. Most of them have very little in life, yet they have much more than what the Ted Turners and Gore Vidals of the world have.

Life has humbled these people. They have few pretensions. What they have to offer the world is their sorrows, hurts, and incredible faith. They are some of the most caring, loving people I've known.

Go to an African American church worship on Sunday morning and experience the joy there, and you'll see what I mean.

Whole cities and groups of people can be deemed losers. I know; I'm from Detroit. Mitch Albom, the best-selling writer and award-winning columnist for *The Detroit Free Press*, laments that the rest of the country views Detroit as gum on the shoes of America.

How wrong they are.

As noted earlier in this book, have a car breakdown in Detroit, and someone will be at your side within minutes offering assistance. I know. Marge and I have had such experiences a number of times over the decades we've lived here. Practically every person who lives in this area reports similar acts of kindness. I don't think that would happen in glamorous cities like Washington, D.C., Seattle, Denver, or L.A.

I guess when no one loves them; losers tend to love each other.

Lest anyone think that they aren't losers in life, just wait. You will discover that we are all Selmas, and we all live in cities like Detroit. If a person lives long enough, he or she will inexorably lose everything—mobility, sight, teeth, continence, reasoning, self-respect, money, friends, and finally life itself. Even our legacy will be forgotten.

Marge, her sister, and I were cleaning out my mother-in-law's home in Rhode Island years ago. Doug, her husband, had died years before. I was removing from one of the walls diplomas and plaques that Doug had received over the years as tributes to his achievements in life. We were throwing them out.

I thought to myself, *So this is where a lifetime of achievement ends, in the trash.*

Losers and fools don't get very far in the evolutionary fight for love and glory. I don't think my career would have gone very far, nor would I have gotten many responses from a profile on e-Harmony, had I described myself as a loser and a fool.

I wonder how many people would venture into a church that informs them on the signage, "Losers and Fools Welcome Here." Or how about, "Leave Your Pretensions at the Door."

I would be the first one through the door. And I know that there would be a lot of people behind me. We would all be connected and bonded together by our broken and wounded conditions, eager to love and support each other.

It's very hard for people to own up to their fears, inadequacies, insecurities, mistakes, and shortcomings. They want to be noticed, to be important. They want to be like Ted Turner and Gore Vidal: successful, on-top-of-things, and having the pick of the genetic litter. They are the Masters of the Universe. Their pictures appear in the newspaper and in magazines. They're on television. Almost everyone knows their names. Their genes will go on forever. They are winners. They have perfected the art of self-glorification. They don't need help; they are doing just fine, thank you very much. They don't pay homage to God. People pay homage to them. That is how it should be, at least for them.

"He is a self-made man and worships his creator." (John Bright) That is their religion.

The question God asks a lot of people is whether they're willing to look like a fool. St. Paul described himself as a fool for Christ. St. Francis of Assisi said that God called him to be a new kind of fool.

I once attended a Christian renewal weekend, and at the close of it, I was given a cross to wear around my neck. After months of delay, I finally worked up the courage to wear it outside of my clothes when I attend church worship on Sunday mornings. I will occasionally run an errand or two after church. I force myself to keep the cross in plain view. I'm fearful that people will view me negatively when they see me wearing it. I don't want to look like a fool.

Some day, I might work up the courage to wear it in full view for everyone to see for a week or more. I wonder if I can handle that.

William F. Buckley, Jr. said, "If you mention God twice at a New York City dinner party, you won't be invited back."

Winston Churchill said, "Courage is rightly esteemed the first of all human qualities because it is the quality which guarantees all others."

It takes a lot of courage to look like a fool.

If Gore Vidal thinks Christian tenets are silly, he must consider as absolutely laughable the belief that the wafer and wine that many Christians receive at Mass each Sunday is the actual body and blood of Jesus Christ, and by receiving it, they are assured of eternal life. Talk about looking like a fool; that is exactly what I believe.

I, like everyone else, need to be affirmed and validated regularly in order to have the strength to affirm and validate others. Yes, Marge and others provide me with much of that strength, but the source that sustains me the most is the Holy Eucharist. When I take the Communion, I know that the source of all affirmation and validation is within me and becomes a part of me. That is all the affirmation and validation I need. I can now give it to the world.

The Holy Eucharist is the last thing in this world that I would give up.

I pray for people regularly. These are people who need help. Prayer, on the surface, seems rather foolish. The outcomes don't seem to be much different than what would occur by pure chance. Yet something remarkable happens to me when I pray for someone. I feel a bond to them that is akin to love. I have prayed for people whom I have never met, yet I feel as close to them as I do my own family.

If prayer doesn't work, then love doesn't work, for prayer is an act of love.

Do the recipients of prayers feel that love, and do those feelings provide them the relief they seek? I believe so. I have been on the receiving end of prayers, and it gave me the "home court advantage," with everyone pulling for me to win the game.

I always like to include in my prayers prayers for people whom I don't like. I won't say my negative feelings toward them turn to love, but those feelings definitely soften.

Are specific prayer requests answered? I believe that they are, and then some.

The blind see, the lame walk, the deaf hear, and the dead are brought back to life.

If that sounds ridiculous, the reader should try this on for size. Occasionally, while I'm praying for people, a string of names unknown to me will pop into my head. I feel compelled to recite them and to ask for their petitions.

Are there real persons and real needs behind these names, or not? I choose to believe that the answer is yes.

If nothing else, it makes my prayer time more interesting.

The descriptive words: loser and fool may be misnomers here. Innocence might be the better word and idea. It's having the innocence to see the world in a new and fresh way, in a way that can make a person look foolish and silly.

The third person of the Trinity is the Holy Spirit. He's not talked about too much in Christian circles. That's too bad, as he's a very cool person. He's the Lord and Giver of life. He's at times referred to as The Sustainer (of life).

There's not a lot of life in the world. Oh, lots of people are eating, talking, playing, and moving from one task to another, but a machine can do most of those things. Are people savoring all the wonderful things occurring around them? Mark Twain put it this way: "Dead at twenty, buried at sixty."

One of my favorite movies is *Harold and Maude*. Maude, played by Ruth Gordon, is a concentration camp survivor who lives life to the fullest. Harold, played by Bud Cort, is a depressed young man who is dominated by his mother and who engages in fake suicides and attends funerals. He drives a remodeled hearse. Maude takes him under her wing and teaches him how to live. They drive in stolen cars (Maude doesn't believe in private ownership), rescue a dying tree in the city and transport it to the country for replanting in another person's truck, drive off on a policeman's motorcycle after he stops Maude for speeding, have a picnic lunch in the city junk yard, play tricks on Harold's military uncle who seeks to enlist Harold in the Army, and finally have sex, even though there's a two generation difference in their ages.

At the end of the movie, Maude is dying by her own hand. Harold is grief-stricken and tells Maude that he loves her. Maude smiles, presses Harold's hand, tells him how wonderful that is, and that he must now love more people.

Maude dies, and so does Harold's morose background. He's last seen singing and dancing on the side of a hill.

I have known people who may not be as madcap as Maude but who nevertheless embrace life like her.

My friend Fred, who like Maude isn't overtly religious, always gives me food for our church food pantry when we're together. He was once seriously bitten by a dog and never considered suing the dog's owner. How's that for forgiveness! He and his wife are retired and are entering the Peace Corps.

Another friend, Rita, informs people that as a hospital social worker, her church was the hospital and her flock was the patients there. She ministered to them on physical, social, emotional, and spiritual levels. She's now retired and informs us that her present church is the local soup kitchen and social services program, and her flock is its clients. My nephew Keith does attend church, and his flock is the patients at the hospice center where he volunteers each week.

I know many such ministers who bring light into the world where there is darkness.

I have never met a grandparent who isn't imbued with new life vis-à-vis their grandchildren. The more foolish and silly they act around their grandchildren, the more fun they each have. The grandparents become children again. They lavish love, attention, and gifts on their grandchildren. Their grandchildren can do no wrong. Their foibles, even their mistakes, are a source of joy. Imagine what a wonderful world it would be if everyone treated each other the way grandparents treat their grandchildren.

Everything children have is a gift. They have done nothing to earn the love and gifts bestowed on them, other than be who they are. That doesn't change as we get older. That is one of the most difficult things for people to understand: that life and everything in it is a gift, that people and God love us simply because of who we are.

The most startling thing ever said to me occurred when our parish priest, Fr. Steven Kelly, was visiting me at home following my hip replacement surgery. I told him how overwhelmed I felt by the outpouring of calls, cards, and well wishes I had received from family, friends, and acquaintances. I told him that I didn't feel worthy of all of this love. He quickly said to me, "Joe, you're not worthy. Only Jesus Christ is worthy."

Marge, our two children, and I vacationed regularly at my in-law's beautiful house in Rhode Island. It is an idyllic setting with Newport and its palatial mansions a fifteen minute car ride away, picture postcard villages with seafood restaurants and lobster boats coming and going, sandy beaches, and the feel of New England salt air everywhere. We would return to my in-law's home after a day at the beach, welcomed by a great meal prepared by my mother-in-law and cocktails served up by my father-in-law, who incidentally didn't drink alcohol.

I would occasionally be lying on the beach, luxuriating in the warmth of the sun and sound of the surf, thinking, *How did a Catholic kid raised in a Belgian-Irish family of eight children on the east side of Buffalo end up in such a great place among all of these well-off WASPs?* I didn't feel worthy of being there.

The answer to that question is simple. I'm not worthy, so shut up, enjoy, and be grateful.

I once asked my friend Mike what he would say on the Day of Judgment to warrant his entrance into Paradise. He said he would fall on the mercy of the court and then keep his mouth shut.

I'm sure the Gates of Heaven will swing open for him, and for everyone else like him. These people, you see, have found the secret to living a more fulfilled life.

THAT'S "IT"

Or, The Secret Revealed

Two men went up into the temple to pray, one a Pharisee and the other a tax collector. The Pharisee stood and prayed thus with himself, "God, I thank thee that I am not like other men, extortioners, unjust, adulterers, or even like this tax collector. I fast twice a week, I give tithes of all that I get." But the tax collector, standing far off, would not even lift up his eyes to heaven, but beat his breast, saying, "God, be merciful to me, a sinner!" I tell you, this man went down to his house justified rather than the other...

Luke 18: 10-14

About this time the disciples came to Jesus and asked him who would be the greatest in the kingdom of heaven. Jesus called a child over and had the child stand near him. Then he said, "I promise you this. If you don't change and become like a child, you will never get into

the kingdom of heaven. But if you are as humble as this child, you are the greatest in the kingdom of heaven."
Matthew 18-1-5

John Adams, one of the signers of the American Declaration of Independence and America's second president, wrote, "I believe there is no one principle which predominates in human nature so much in every stage of life, from the cradle to the grave, in males and females, old and young, black and white, rich and poor, high and low, as this passion for superiority . . . every individual is seen to be strongly actuated by a desire to be seen, heard, talked about, approved, and respected." He labeled this a natural "*passion for distinction.*"

Icarus is a character in Greek mythology. King Minos of Crete imprisons him and his father, Daedalus. His father builds wings for himself and Icarus in order to fly to freedom. He used wax and string to fasten feathers to reeds of varying lengths to imitate the curves of birds' wings.

When their wings were ready, Daedalus warned Icarus to fly at medium altitude. If he flew too high, the sun could melt the wax of his wings, and if he flew too low, the sea could dampen the feathers. In both cases, he could fall from the sky and die.

Once they had escaped Crete, Icarus became exhilarated by flight. Ignoring his father's warnings, he flew higher and higher. The sun melted the wax holding his wings together, and the boy fell into the water and drowned.

Humans are like Icarus, and they must heed the advice of Daedalus in order to fly successfully through life. They must maintain a medium altitude, not flying too high or too low.

Each act of self-glorification, self-righteousness, and self-justification brings them closer and closer to the sun, melting away more and more wax, and bringing them nearer to their downfall and demise.

Each act of self-reproach and abasement brings them closer and closer to the water, dampening their wings and bringing them nearer to their downfall and demise.

They maintain a medium altitude by believing in themselves, while at the same time questioning and challenging themselves.

Solely affirming oneself leads to egotism while always questioning and criticizing oneself can lead to discouragement and defeatism. Alone, they destroy the human spirit; together they embolden it.

It is the resolution of this confusing duality that brings forth the incredible potential for love and achievement that humans possess.

About twenty years ago Coca-Cola introduced New Coke. New Coke was a reformulation of Classic Coke, which had been the company's mainstay. New Coke flopped. The public wanted Classic Coke. Coca-Cola quickly pulled New Coke from the store shelves and brought back Classic Coke.

In explaining this enormous corporate mistake and near disaster, the CEO for Coca-Cola said in part, "We're not that smart, nor are we that dumb."

That's a good motto for humans to have:

I'm not that smart, nor am I that dumb.

I'm not that good, nor am I that bad.

Dave the builder told me that in order to build a solid structure he must insure that water doesn't enter it. To build a more fulfilled life, we must insure that becoming self-centered doesn't seep in and destroy our good and noble instincts and intentions. That is the enemy that must be defeated. When that enemy is defeated, the wings of angels that humans possess will take them to great and sustainable heights.

What does it mean to have a fulfilled life? The *American Heritage Dictionary* definition of the word "fulfill" is, "to bring into actuality." A fulfilled life is an actualized life. It is living a life that is both being and becoming, where a person is both comfortable with him or herself is also always striving to be a better person.

This can happen when a person has shaken off the shackles of self-glorification and its ugly companions through contrition and humility. A person is then free to be and to enjoy him or herself, while at the same time striving to be their best. It's a life where a person eagerly takes in the world around him or her. It's a life of caring, compassion, and love. It's also a life of creative involvement and worthwhile achievements.

It is out with the false self and in with the true self.

It's the life everyone wants to live, and can live.

Jesus tells us to take the last seat, and assures us that the last will come first and the first will come last. We must possess the innocence and humility of a child to be happy and fulfilled. He's telling us that happiness results from a contrite heart and a humble spirit.

"The Lord is nigh unto them that are of a contrite heart, and will save such as be of a humble spirit."
Psalm 34-18

Contrition is the awareness that we deliberately or inadvertently hurt other people by our thoughts, words, and actions. We are sorry we hurt others.

Humility is the awareness that we frequently "darken counsel by words without knowledge." It's being aware that we don't know nearly as much as we think we know and that we have limited control over our lives.

There is nothing more humbling than looking like a fool, yet that is precisely what a person must sometimes do in order to achieve happiness and success. I, for instance, struggled with the writing of this book when I feared that it would be a flop and I would look like a fool. That obstacle abated when I was able to say to myself, "Yes, it may be a flop, and I might look like the biggest jerk in the world. That's okay. I will follow my instincts rather than succumb to my fears."

In the movie, *Zorba The Greek*, Alan Bates plays the rigid Basil, and Anthony Quinn plays the free-spirited Zorba. They join in a business enterprise wherein they construct a wooden structure that will transport timber down the side of a hill. Opening day arrives, with the townspeople looking on and the bishop blessing the apparatus. The first logs begin to slowly descend the hill. They soon pick up speed and come roaring down, with the structure collapsing behind it and the on-lookers scurrying for cover. Basil is devastated as he and Zorba survey the wreckage. His dreams and plans are in ruin.

Zorba, who like Maude, has an unquenchable *joie de vivre*, slaps Basil on the back and proclaims, "Basil, wasn't it a magnificent crash?"

Zorba knows how to turn defeat into triumph.

If this book tanks, I hope I can tell people that it was a magnificent failure. I can put it on my *What Was I Thinking?* list.

There's a scene in the movie, *Annie Hall,* in which Woody is talking to an impressionable college woman who's rhapsodizing on the spiritual qualities of an enlightened guru, who they see exiting the men's room and adjusting his belt. She finishes her paean by declaring him as a god. Woody wryly comments that her god has just left the men's room.

Ernest Becker observes in his Pulitzer Prize winning book, *The Denial of Death,* that humans can soar to sublime heights with their god-like qualities but are constantly reminded of their vulnerability, mortality, and limitations through the bodily function of defecation.

You will see a lot of copulating on movie screens, occasional urinating, but you'll never see any defecating. Movie producers don't want to remind their viewers of their humanness.

The need to defecate makes contrite and humble humans of us all.

Telling ourselves to be contrite and humble is like telling ourselves to be happy or loving. It's a great concept but how is it done, especially when it runs against the human grain of self-glorification? It is not something that comes natural to humans.

I've been an exerciser my whole life. It has never come easy for me. In fact, I must force myself to do it. I do it because of the good things it does for me.

Contrition and humility might come easy to some people, but for most of us, it's a foreign substance that the body wants to reject.

Below is a simple mental exercise that when consistently practiced I believe will result in increasing a person's contrition and humility quotient.

This program is counterintuitive. It is equivalent to being injected with a germ for the purpose of preventing that germ from later invading our body and destroying it.

Tape the following six one-sentence statements to any surface that you look at regularly. Recite them to yourself. You will slowly internalize them, loosening the shackles of self-glorification.

THE CODE OF CONTRITION AND HUMILITY

1) I'm not as nice as I think I am.
I want to be nice. I try to be nice. I'm even nice much of the time. That's about it. Be forgiving and seek goodness.

2) I'm not as smart as I think I am.
I want to be smart. I study hard to be knowledgeable. I even say and do many things that are smart. That's about it. Be forgiving and seek goodness.

3) I'm not as honest as I think I am.
I generally play by the rules of the game, but when the referees aren't looking I'm apt to be dishonest. Be forgiving and seek goodness.

4) I don't deserve most of the things I possess.
I have talents and I've worked hard to develop them and to succeed, but most of the good things in my life have fallen into my lap. Be forgiving and seek goodness.

5) I'm willing to risk making a fool of myself.
If following your dreams, vision, even your intuitions, means looking like a fool, then look like a fool. It probably

means you're on to something big and wonderful. Be forgiving and seek goodness.

6) I, and the people I know and love, may not be alive in a month.
Cherish every person and moment in life as if it were the last opportunity you will have with that person and live those moments to the fullest. Be forgiving and seek goodness.

It won't take long before you own these statements. When these six statements are fixed in your mind and are playing out in your behavior, replace them with this single statement: *Be contrite and humble today.*

Combine this cognitive exercise with an equally simple behavioral exercise.

1) Casually tell people something that you have been hiding from others. It might be a medical or emotion condition: "I'm under treatment for hypertension." I'm being treated for anxiety or depression." "I'm an alcoholic, or a sex addict, or a compulsive shopper." "I have a hard time controlling my temper." It might be an embarrassing social problem: "I just got demoted, or, fired from my job." "I'm unemployed." "I'm working my way out of debt." "I spend too much." "I'm difficult

to live with." "I always have to have my way." "I should spend much more time with my wife (kids)."

2) Don't always defend yourself when you make mistakes or hurt another person: "I'm sorry I did that." "That was a stupid thing for me to do." "Please forgive me." "What was I thinking?"

3) Admit when you're confused and need help: "How do you do this?" "Tell me what I'm doing wrong." "Thanks for helping me out. I couldn't have done it without your help." "How do I get there?" "God, I need your help."

As you undertake these cognitive and behavioral exercises, fill the angel wings you possess with the air of personal affirmations. Give yourself credit for having the courage to change and for working hard at it. Remind yourself of your successes in life and the tremendous value you have as a human being. Celebrate the gifts that you bring into the world.

Celebrate the New You!

Fly out of your prison of being self-centered and to freedom.

Adding a seventh statement can accelerate this process. This statement takes a huge amount of humility because it says I'm not in complete control of my life. It reads:

7) *God help me to have a contrite spirit and a humble heart.*
What I can't do, God can.

"But I don't believe in God," you might say. That's OK. I don't believe that a multi-ton plane can stay up in the sky, yet I fly on them. I don't believe the earth can stay perfectly in orbit, yet I make future plans. I don't believe self-centered humans can love and care for other humans, yet it happens all the time. I don't believe people can change, yet that also happens a lot. I don't believe that historians can write fact-filled history books, yet I read them all the time. I can't believe Magellan circumnavigated the world with almost nothing to guide him, yet he did it. I can't believe that I did ninety push-ups and ninety-five sit-ups this morning, yet I did them. I can't believe that I'm writing this book, yet here it is.

Step into the mystery of life.

Besides, virtually nobody totally believes or disbelieves in the existence of God. It's a shifting blend of conviction and doubt. It's those shifting shades of gray that John F. Kennedy spoke about. So make the above statement with whatever percentage of belief in a Higher Power that lays within you, even if it's in the single digits. You might wish to change the statement to:

7) *God, who I suspect doesn't exist, please help me to acquire a contrite heart and a humble spirit.*

The rewards for having a contrite heart and a humble spirit are manifold.

Contrite and humble people know what they like and go with those likes. They have little need for status symbols or to "keep up with the Joneses." They therefore tend to live within their means, which affords them financial security and considerable peace of mind. They are great communicators because they are less interested in calling attention to themselves and are more interested in what others have to say. They are good listeners who can empathize with how others are feeling. They are open and honest with their own feelings, and this opens the door for others to convey their thoughts and feelings to them. They are socially popular because they validate and affirm others, and this attracts people to them.

They tend to be physically healthy because they're not "on stage" all the time, which greatly reduces stress in their lives, and this results in benefits to their cardiovascular, immune, and organ systems.

They are fun to be around because they will frequently poke fun at themselves, and never at others. They are full of gratitude because they are aware of how much has been given them in their life. They are generous because they wish to share these blessings with others who are less fortunate. They are productive and efficient because they will acknowledge what they don't know and will seek advice from others in solving problems and use that advice. They surprise and impress others because they are frequently underestimated. They strive for perfection because they are keenly aware of their imperfections.

They are emotionally healthy because they can let go of their hurts through forgiveness. They build solid and long-lasting relationships because they will apologize for their mistakes and not carry grudges. They tend to have deep spiritual and religious roots because they recognize and ask for help from a Higher Power in making it through this difficult world and in achieving their potential.

Overall, they toss off the masks that their false self has been wearing, that have become so burdensome. Their true self emerges, and with it freedom, joy, and the blossoming of their God-given gifts.

They live fulfilled lives.

There is one sure test to determine if a person has a contrite heart and a humble spirit. People feel wanted and valued when in their presence.

These special people can be the person you talk to at a party, in the grocery line, at your desk. You're not sure what he or she did or said that makes you feel so good about yourself. It might be their welcoming body language, the things they remembered about you, their interest in what's been happening in your life, their smile when you tell them the good things in your life, their sadness when you tell them about your misfortunes, their touch on your arm.

They possess a peaceful glow that relaxes and warms you.

There is nothing pretentious about them. They don't stand out in the crowd. If you asked them what their secret is, they probably couldn't say.

They have the secret to living a more fulfilled life. They have a contrite heart and a humble spirit.

They can easily be you, anyone, or me.

I once was watching the Special Olympics. The event was a foot race. As the runners were rounding the track, one of them stumbled and fell. The other runners saw the collapsed runner, stopped running, and went back to help him.

That's a taste of what the room labeled heaven is like. It's definitely worth checking out.

REFERENCES

Connie Zweig and Jeremiah Abrams, eds., <u>Meeting The Shadow: The Hidden Power of the Dark Side of Human Nature</u>. (G.P. Putnam's Sons, 1990) M. Scott Peck, <u>Healing Human Evil</u> p 176.

3665420

Made in the USA